Anonymous

Hand Book to the City of Little Rock, State of Arkansas

Popularly styled

Anonymous

Hand Book to the City of Little Rock, State of Arkansas
Popularly styled

ISBN/EAN: 9783337419493

Printed in Europe, USA, Canada, Australia, Japan

Cover: Foto ©Andreas Hilbeck / pixelio.de

More available books at **www.hansebooks.com**

CITY OF LITTLE ROCK ARKANSAS

From The Arkansas Gazette,
January 15, 1897.

�֍ ✶ ✶

.

Published under the
AUSPICES OF THE
LITTLE ROCK BOARD
OF TRADE.

✶ ✶ ✶

WRITE TO LITTLE
ROCK BOARD OF TRADE
FOR SUCH INFORMA-
TION AS DOES NOT
APPEAR IN THIS HAND
BOOK.

✶ ✶ ✶

THE LITTLE ROCK
BOARD OF TRADE OF-
FERS SUBSTANTIAL
INDUCEMENTS TO MAN
UFACTURERS TO LO-
CATE IN THE CITY.

✶ ✶ ✶

PRESS OF
GAZETTE PUBLISHING COMPANY,
LITTLE ROCK, ARK.

INTRODUCTION.

HAVING IN MIND authenticated accounts of Arkansas and her chief city, nothing is more remarkable to strangers, who study either of the two, than the lack of manufactures and of railway facilities, called for by favoring conditions of the State. It is not a question with them, whether on the one hand watercourses and present railroad connections, or whether on the other hand, extraneous causes enter into the case, but what have the people of Arkansas and of Little Rock engaged in, that so great opportunities should have escaped notice?

ABSENCE OF RAILROADS AND FACTORIES.

There are of course reasons for the absences of railroads and manufactures, equal to the resources and advantages of the state; however on first thought, it were impossible to name any one in particular. But it is, surely, not a sufficient answer to the question, to say, that both Little Rock and the state, are cut off from other avenues to wealth and greatness, than that of agriculture, even though eight-tenths or more of Arkansas' population engage in farming. Such an answer involves the hypothesis of the Arkansan being, so to speak, insular in his conception of means to ends, when in fact his hospitality to new ideas and his liberality and enterprise in trials of merit with his neighbors have for years won for his state the applause of all sister commonwealths of the Union.

The reason is to be sought further. Arkansas and Little Rock may not have thought so before times, but there are causes for the lack of manufactures and railroads other than appear on the surface, and for which an explanation must be sought in the history of other Southern states. In the case of Georgia and her capital city, it is supplied in the fact of powerful Wall Street friends whose enthusiasm over resources of the state, by reason of its disinterestedness and sincerity, stimulated investments in mines, factories, railroads, quarries and town property. In the case of Virginia it is found in the patronage of strong railway corporations, who hesitated at no expense, and who left no means untried to bring capital and population to the development of their territory. In the case of Alabama it is found directly in railway construction on the part of the state government, after which it was easy with railroad capitalists and manufactures not only to reason for liberality and enterprise on the part of the legislature, but for the confidence of its people in the resources and advantages of their state. And in the case of the Carolinas it is that of Providence helping those who help themselves, which, interpreted in their history, means that having continued to join modest earnings of the farm, shop, store and professions, there has been effected results which represent an aggregate in-

vestment of local capital to the amount of
millions.

Hence, however, the instances cited
only complicate the maze. Arkansas and
Little Rock must follow if they are to
enter upon the development of railroads
and manufactures, in one, or it might be
in all of them is to be found the clew.
Excepting friends who are strongly en-
trenched in the confidence of Wall Street
(but which with proper approach can be
furnished in the person of three distin-
guished railway magnates)—Arkansas
possesses all means supplied by the
states named. And what is better, in her
coal fields, water power, navigable water
courses, forests, marbles, building stone,
manganese, antimony, beauxite, zinc, copper, lead, chalk, gypsum, green sand,
marl, fruit, grass, grain, and cotton lands,
she supplies in her own territory more
than the aggregate resources and advantages of the five states combined.

AN INTERESTING EXAMPLE.

Separating the subject of manufactures
from that of railroads, it is of course unreasonable to expect, upon a considerable
scale, industrial development, without
leaders possessed of business experience
and judgment sufficient to attract general confidence; or who, at least, add to
the organization and promotion of manufacturing enterprises, skilled knowledge,
if not time and money, as evidence of
good faith.

Take the Georgia cotton mills for example. Though afterwards carried to
heights rivalling states deemed to have
a monopoly of cotton manufacture, its
history, no doubt, turns upon the Augusta factory, situated at Augusta, Ga.
And to admit that much, is to bring into
the light the forgotten fact, that the
whole system, as a profitable investment
for that state, turned upon the skilled
knowledge and industry of one man,
(Cogin by name) who, immediately an-
tedating the war of the states, was called
to the management of the Augusta factory. It was he who, not only carried
the enterprise to a paying basis for the
first time in its history, but whose genius became established in the cotton
world, immediately after the war, in almost fabulous earnings for which the
mill is celebrated.

There had been nothing to parallel it
in the cotton mill industry of the state,
and nothing, in the situation at the time,
to invite great cotton plants. And, therefore, once it was shown, that nothing
militated against their encouragment and
success, excepting inexperience, lack of
capital, and lack of industrial leaders,
not only was local capital from many

sources combined for investment in cotton mills, but when approached by the right men, industrial capitalists of the East were not slow to invest in Georgia cotton mills. And in fact, when the moral of it all is sought for, it will be found in a proviso which obtained in both cases, that those placed in charge should be of similar training and experience to that of the man who, in all truth, can be said to have created the great cotton mill industry of the South, when from comparative nothingness he raised the fame of the Augusta Factory, as a money-maker, to that of the best in the world.

RAILROADS ALIVE TO THE SITUATION.

As in the case of manufactures upon their own merit, so it is when the interest of railroads in the matter, is joined to the subject of the industrial development in the state and at its capital city. One of the systems at last has in mind results which will follow when the opportunity of the two becomes understood, but at the same time, being always under the suspicion of working for selfish ends, it has been at sea, as to the best course to pursue.

It has hesitated to proceed unnecessarily in a wrong direction, and in consequence, has held itself in abeyance, until delay, in the promotion of manufactures, has become irksome, if not detrimental to its interests, with this result, that it is impatient enough to move independently in the matter. And herein it is, that a serious disadvantage can follow such establishment of industries, conditioned to resources of the state. For if the railroads are, perforce, required to take the initiative, Little Rock will in effect, lose the command of its own affairs and the railroads of course, farm out to strangers favors and advantages necessary to the success of manufacturing plants.

Of the interest, old, new, and projected roads, feel in the outcome of local development directed to manufactures; it is not necessary to add that it does not, in toto, depend upon the prospect of an "in and out" haul of material found in their territory. It also involves both the settlement of the country, and a better distribution of money over their territory (not to mention, on account of aggregated manufactures under such conditions), a greater business out of Little Rock, than would be possible at any point in the Southwest, outside of St. Louis, Kansas City, and New Orleans.

FROM THE STANDPOINT OF LITTLE ROCK.

Predisposed as the facts of the case are, to the direct question of Little Rock's future history, there is but one answer: That of a manufacturing center, though at the same time it must always remain the largest and wealthiest commercial, social, educational, and political center of the state.

It is a result which is to follow, however, an honest mistake upon the part of its leaders, for a time, kept out of sight resources and opportunities which, in the case of other cities of its size and population, would have ultimated in one of the largest manufacturing centers of the Southern States. And in the sense that it is an unavoidable consequence, if business considerations are to govern its fortunes, Little Rock need not be impatient of its realization, if sponsors appear for it in centers of industrial capital, provided similar efforts are made to overcome inexperience in manufacture, as took place when the people of Augusta, Ga., placed their great factory under the direction of the famous mill man from the state of Maine.

The conditions, not to say variety and extent of native material, are so much in its favor, that, at a venture, it can be said to have no parallel on the Western Continent. This refers not only to cheap fuel at the present time, but to cheaper fuel still from coal mines lately discovered clo e at hand. It refers also to cotton and woolen mills, oil mills, leather manufacture, aluminum plants, agricultural implements, reduction works for zinc, lead, and copper, paper mills, car shops, wagon factories, furniture factories, good schools, good health, good water, favoring social conditions to mill owners and mill workers; and next to manifold and unlimited means to success, native to the state, it presents at the present time, with a prospect of becoming greater still at an early day, the largest, ready made market close at hand, of any originating center in the Union, of less than a quarter million of inhabitants.

Or in other words, not only do the facts of the case prove an opportunity for investing capital which carries with it predisposing causes that mean prosperity, but an importance, which is to round itself short of no manufacturing center of the South—with all railroads in operation, and all new road bending their influence and encouragement to the promotion of enterprises sure to give them a large busine s; and sure to bring to their immediate territory, a commercial and social development commensurate with the character and excellence of the country.

In the same connection, not to be misunderstood, it should perhaps be said that though it may not be in general, so known to the public, it is in evidence against Little Rock that in striving for commercial honors, it is in the end seen, that splendid city as it is, it has not grown to a commanding height in size and population. The fact is, an avoidance of manufacture was but natural, at a day when returns from commercial investments in the state, paid four or five times the amount derived from other forms of business enterprises. But now, that such a day is gone, the past returns to incite a new prospec, of prosperity. That of industries which cannot promise less than a means to gain, depended upon a safe basis, at the same time it can be expected to add four and five times the number of people to the sum total of population, than followed when commercial enterprise was only in force.

— — —

SPONSOR FOR LITTLE ROCK AND THE STATE.

Respecting the offices of well known railway magnates as sponsors for Little Rock and the state: It is in evidence that incalculable benefit would follow the selection of at least one of them, for the reason that it would aid in undoing much misapprehension of Arkansas, and at the same time benefit properties in which he is directly interested. But, transcending any selfish interest in the matter, the man contemplated in this connection can be moved as well from the side of public spirit and an opportunity to distinguish himself as a benefactor, not only to a state, but to a great section of our common country where, nature itself, pleads the cause of a brave and generous people. For however any effort toward the successful development of manufactures, must turn, primarily, upon great aggregates of native material, to satisfy capitalists of the safety and profit of their investment, like the motion imparted to things when Fort Smith and the state woke up in 1887, the influence would reach, irresistibly, to all Southern and Southwestern states of the Union; and the genius of the man, for directing great enterprises, become crowned by a fame for usefulness to his fellow man second to no American citizen of the present day.

It is not a fruitless or impracticable step to take. John H. Inman alone proved that it was in keeping with the requiremens of capitalists who learn, comparatively, nothing of inviting fields for investment that lie beyond the hard grind of business which leaves them scarcely time to cultivate the acquaintance of their own family. And if successful in the case of Atlanta and the state of Georgia, why not in the case of Little Rock and the state of Arkansas, whose manifold and unlimited native material equal the natural resources of at least four manufacturing states of the South?

Again: If from desire on his part to avoid publicity, or any other reason, it is discovered that this man, most fitted of all others for the sponsorship, is disinclined to lead in the matter (for at best it will be no child's play to be left off when the actor has had his fun), there is recourse left in a convocation of railway magnates, boards of trade, and state authorities, who can line up their effort in parallel directions; and as need for it presents itself, the party of the first part, resident at money centers, identify those publicly selected to invite manufactures to the state and its capital city. The only objection to this plan, as compared to the first, is the fact that it would lack the stamp of individuality, or original conception, which at any turn of the game, would show the same directing hand and brain, and therefore at all times inspire confidence by reason of consistency both in the design and in its execution. But it is better than nothing at all, and if it is, perforce, the only alternative left to our state authorities and the Little Rock Board of Trade, it is at least to that extent a point gained from which, thereafter, it would be possible to discover advantagse that would not otherwise appear to those who, for the first time, undertake the establishment of factories.

RAILWAY AVENUES TO RAW MATERIAL.

Of roads, present and prospective, over which it is possible to concentrate upon Little Rock, all native material of the state, it is not necessary to emphasize the fact that they are also direct and indirect means over which to reach markets of the West, Southwest and Mexico, not to mention markets of the South, where the predilection already exists of patronizing home industries.

It is an advantage, both as respects a supply of native material and of connections to ready made markets not possible to another point in the trans-Mississippi division of the Union. There are other points to which more trunk roads have already been constructed, than Little Rock could hope for in the next twenty-five years, however, all other things may come her way. But there is none of them whose railway lines command so many kinds, and so great a supply of native material at short range, none of them, at which the cost of material, to begin with, would be lower to manufactures; and, therefore, none of them, the outcome of which would pair with conditions favoring Litt e Rock, in competing at first hand, for the manufacturing trade before described.

It is also extraordinary that so little has been understood of the situation, both upon the score of railway lines in operation to Little Rock, and of others in sight. Of the first, railways in operation, there are three systems or groups which, in effect, means (trunk lines, branches and connections operated in this state) twenty-s ven roads that connect Little Rock to so many different parts of the state.

The operated roads are as follows, viz.: Missouri Pacific railway, north; Missouri Pacific railway, south; Little Rock and Memphis, branch of the Missouri Pacific; Little Rock and Alexandria, or Houston, Central Arkansas and Northern railway; Cotton Belt railway, north; Cotton Belt railway, South; Altheimer branch of the Cotton Belt rai way; Little Rock and Memphis railway; Pike City connection of the Missouri Pacific railway; Prescott and Wallaceburg connection of the Missouri Pacific railway; Arkadelphia and Dalark connection of the Missouri Pacific railway; Hoxie and Pocahontas connection of the Missouri Pacific and Nettleton systems; Russellville and Dardane le connection of the Missouri Pacific railway; Searcy and West Point connection of the Mi-souri Pacific railway; Warren, Eldorado, Nashville, Greenwood and Batesville branches of the Missouri Pacific railway; Clarendon and Helena connection of the Cotton Belt railway; Rob Roy and English connection of the Cotton Belt rai way; Stu t gart and DeWitt connection of the Cotton Belt railway; Helena, Brinkl y and Indian Bay connection of the Little Rock and Memphis railway; Magnolia and Shreveport branches of the Cotton Belt railway; White and Black River connection of the Missouri Pacific, Little Rock and Memphis, and Cotton Belt railways.

Of roads "in sight" there are three cla ses—extensions and connections of roads now operated, roads now building, and projected roads, viz.: Little Rock and Memphis extension; Mena, Hot Springs and Little Rock branch of the Kansas City, Pittsburg and Gulf railway; Miami, Bentonvil e and Little Rock branch of the Nettleton system; Harrison, Marshall and Little Rock branch of the Mackay road projected from St. Louis to Abilene, Texas, under the title of the St. Louis, Siloam and Southern railway; St. Paul and Little Rock; Mansfield and Little Rock; Eureka Springs and Little Rock; Chadwick and Little

Rock, and the Salem and Little Rock
branches of the St. Louis and San Fran-
cisco railway. And, indeed, of which
last named group of branch roads (two
of which will be but t) it is to be an-
ticipated of their extension, that they
will bring to their territory and to Little
Rock a prosperity unexampled in the history of Southwestern railway development; the remarkable character of the
country penetrated being the vindication
of the prediction made.

OUR RAILWAY AUTHORITIES NOT POSTED.

In connection with the subject of native material for manufactures, to be
alone derived from territory of the Missouri Pacific railway, there is one difficulty in the way, which, without extraneous help, it will not be easy to overcome. It is this: Though facts of the
case may be, in a general way, argued
by the mileage so great a system op-
erates in this state, so extraordinary are the amounts, and so wide-
ranged the variety of material, that, in
any serious attempt at details, investors
are, on first impulse, inclined to hold
such information at arm's length. It is
not due to any indisposition to take hold
of a good thing, when they know it, but
being at best strangers to the state, it
seems to them, incredible, that others in
position to do so, had not, in time, pre-
occupied the ground floor to the exclusion of all outsiders.

In the same connection, that of material to be derived by Little Rock from
territory of the Missouri Pacific railway,
it is of course presumed, that the authorities of the road are sufficient to establish such information of the country penetrated, as would impress itse f, but they
have accompli-hed nothing in that direction. There is no doubt of their interest in the development and profitable operation of the road in their Arkansas territory, and upon the whole, they have
authorized most liberal expenditures to
advertise the state along with matters
of their own. But when inquiry is
pushed further than this, it is found
that they have had neither the inclination to study the country, upon original
grounds of their own, nor the leisure to
study information, supplied by their
subordinates, which established the fact
that, outside of timber and farm products, there is not ten miles square in
their territory which does not supply
native material required in manufactures and the arts. And as the same
condition applies to other roads, as it
does to the Missouri Pacific, at a glance
there is seen plenty of reason for collect-
ing data, necessary to a proper authenti-

cation of Little Rock's present and future prospects as a manufacturing center, whether the outcome is to be propitiated by means of sponsors, by independent action, or by means of a convocation of railway magnates, boards of trade, and state authorities.

WIDE EXTENT OF TERRITORY.

That the variety and extent of material found in the Arkansas territory, of present and prospective railroads, is not al. on paper, nor all in the air, take the following named counties penetrated by them.

Territory of the Missouri Pacific railway, main line, branches and direct connections: Clay, Lawrence, Jackson, Independence, White, Lonoke, Pulaski, Saline, Hot Springs, Garland, Clark, Nevada, Hempstead, Miller, Howard, Ouachita, Union, Bradley, Drew, Ashley, Desha, Lincoln, Jefferson, Phil ips, Lee, St. Francis, Cross, Craighead, Woodruff, Faulkner, Conway, Pope, Johnson, Franklin, Sebastian, Crittenden and Pike counties.

Territory of the Cotton Belt railway, and immediate connections: Green, Clay, Craighead, Cross, Woodruff, Monroe, Arkansas, Jefferson, Cleveland, Dallas, Calhoun, Ouachita, Columbia, Lafayette, Miller, Lonoke, Pulaski and Phi lips.

Counties reached by the Little Rock and Memphis railway: Pulaski, Lonoke, Prairie, Monroe, St. Francis, Crittenden;

Counties to be connected to Litt e Rock by means of the Mena, Hot Springs and Little Rock branch of the Kansas City, Pittsburg and Gulf railway: Benton, Polk, Sevier, Little River, Miller, Montgomery, Garland and Saline.

Territory the propo ed branch road from the Nettleton system will connect to Little Rock: Fulton, Sharp, Lawrence, Craighead, Crittenden, Benton, Madison, Johnson, Logan, Yell, Garland, Perry and Saline counties.

Territory of the Mansfield and Little Rock branch of the Frisco: Seba tian, Scott, Logan, Yell, and Perry counties.

Territory of the Salem and Litt e Rock branch of the Frisco railway: Fulton, Izard, Independence, and White counties.

Territory of the New Orleans and Northwestern: Ashley, Bradley, Dallas, Grant and Saline counties.

Territory of the St. Louis, Siloam and Southern railway: Marion, Boone, Newton, Franklin, Crawford, Sebastian, Searcy, Van Buren and Faulkner counties.

But this is not all. Not only does the given territory supp'y, at a glance, a case covering seventy, out of seventyfive, counties in a state remarkable for the variety and extent of its natural resources (and therefore a case for the railroads in which concentration at a certain point would mean a market for material used in manufactures and the arts), but if all three are, hereafter, to be governed by business reasons affecting the one as it does the other, no alternative is left, other than that of joint action (of Little Rock and the state-at-large) with the railroads, along lines of progress called for by exigencies of the situation. And if not that, then is it high time for Arkansas and her chief city, as well as her railroads, to go out of the business of material development, trusting to luck for that which comes only through energy, enterprise, hard thinking, and the good of the one toward the others?

LOCAL ADVANTAGES OF MANUFACTURES.

Of course, given a wide extent of territory upon which to predicate Little Rock's claim to public notice, it were in many respects quite easy to cast a horoscope that would, so to speak, "hold water." But it is a serious question, environed as it is by such strong rivals as Memphis, St. Louis and Kansas City, whether the direction of its energies to commercial enterprise does not in the end militate against its reasonable prospects of wealth and greatness.

It is not meant that the greatest success to commercial enterprise is impossible, other things being equal. But it is a fact that the ruling industries of the state, agriculture, and lumber have not proved, so far, strong enough to sustain a trade superstructure to which, on the surface, it appears entitled.

Its commercial accomplishment is not less possible than in the case of other interior cities of the country, but if there has been any advantage which it does not enjoy, it has been either railroad concentration and patronage, manufactures, or competing rail and river outlet, or a combination of the three, all of which will follow in the course of time for Little Rock. But it has in no case depended upon a greater amount of native material upon which it is practicable to base manufactures, as well as railroad connections, galore; and at the same time retain in their favor, so large a margin of virgin territory upon which to build a splendid commerce.

In the case of manufactures, for which it must take the initiative, if it is to hold its own against rivals, it is quite a different thing. It involves the exchange of commodities for raw material, which in the end builds up two great lines of industries instead of one, or which, in the aggregate contributes to both the commercial and industrial wealth of communities. It becomes the scene of adventure for young people of industrious habits who, while bound by home ties to all parts of the state, find it a means to preferment, whether of skill in mechanics, business management, fame or fortune.

It is also a reciprocal line of industry for any city, in the sense, that for each ten thousand dollars invested in factories, it adds thirty or forty inhabitants to a community, whereas the same amount invested in commerce only adds ten persons.

But best of all: Take the tables on manufactures (extracted from United States census reports for 1890) given in another place. As a creator of local wealth, and the wealth of a state, commerce compares to it, as a peanut stand does to a wholesale grocery house. For instance: In the table of summaries under the head of "Arkansas Manufactures," not only will it be found that the total value of manufactured products aggregated $22,659,179, which was derived for one year, from $10,448,236, in plants, and $4,523,378 in live assets, but of the total cash value of manufactured products, $12,397,261, was distributed, or remained in the state, as cost of material: $5,794,883, as total wages paid; and $1,035,256 as miscellaneous expenses. Or say $19,182,400.

THE HALF HAS NEVER BEEN TOLD.

Regarding the aggregates or amounts of native material: Any other part of this report is an easy task to perform, compared to the difficulties met with in a serious discussion of this branch of the subject. The difficulty does not lie with the subject, or its treatment, but with readers who are strangers to the state, or for the matter of it, with all readers, who have not had to do with the exploitation of this state, or with the application of its natural resources to conditions of manufactures and commerce.

Had the state been situated closer to the beaten highways of the Union, and the general business man and traveler oftener a visitor to its midst, nothing more would have been needed to establish the facts in the case, than their publication in so many words and figures. But in this instance, when it is considered, that nothing had gone before in public print, or in the general knowledge of the public, on which to rely for conclusions in the premises, something of the reader's indulgence must be entreated until the subject has been rounded to the end, and the writer, at the same time understood, as only performing that part of a chronicler of facts covering the fortunes of a state and city unknown to them, or mayhap, only known to them in a sense which has nothing to do with the question treated.

In plain, it is a case in which possibilities inhering to natural resources of the country, read much like an imposition upon the credulity of the public. And indeed, it is a case in which a change to the other horn of the dilemma has no better effect. For if substantiated in a manner otherwise satisfactory to the reader, the tendency is to shame their understanding of a country well worth their notice; and therefore, also establish for a people who were entitled to consideration, if upon no other ground than the character of country selected by them, as a home for themselves and their posterity.

TWO HUNDRED AND FIFTY BILLIONS FEET OF LUMBER.

For example of what has been just said, take the forest area of the state: It is reasonably estimated to be twenty-five millions of acres in extent. This means, at only 6,000 feet to the acre, (which is the minimum estimate for merchantable forest in Arkansas) the sum of one hundred and fifty billions of feet of timber, suited to manufactures and commerce. But, instead of one hundred and fifty billions of feet, the amount of stumpage is in all reason two-thirds greater. This is self-evident. For if there is taken into account the density of forest in the low-ground, hardwood districts of the state, where measurements often run to 14,000 feet to the acre, and in true pine districts of the state, where measurements run to 12,000 feet to the acre (the area of the two being more than equal to the remainder of the state), at a glance there is had, two hundred and fifty billions of feet, which is the greatest amount of timber found in any other state of the Union.

Another complicating phase of the subject, under the head of timber resources, upon which, for manufactures and construction, Little Rock new draws, and is hereafter to draft her needs, is found in the compilation of forest statistics (U. S. Census Reports on Arkansas), as compared to facts in the case. They are so far out of line with what has been practically established on behalf of the state, as to put a doubtful construction upon the entire volume devoted to forest areas of the Union. So to speak, the compilers "fell down," because they either did not know their business, or because their information was obtained, at second hand, from persons who were ignorant of what they talked, or who, being designing 'and sharks, hoped by such misrepresentation to shut out mil. owners for a time, or who hoped to keep out buyers likely to compete against parties by whom they were employed.

COAL RESOURCES OF THE STATE.

Though under different aspects, the same reasoning toward those who are strangers to the state, applies to coal discoveries made in the state. And, by way of parenthesis, it may be said to apply to everything else in the state, the exploitation of which had been entrusted to other hands, than those whose experience in our western country, leads them to discard theories, and get down to "business," if they wish to make discoveries of value to commerce, manufactures and the arts.

Not only has the coal area of the state served to raise a conflict between statements authorized by the government through the United States geological survey, and statements authorized by the state through the Arkansas geological survey, ended some years ago, but it is proved, that in neither case had the facts of the system been reached. And the matter in question, therefore, still hanging fire for no other reason than the mistakes, or shall we call it, "errors" of science.

In the case of the first named survey, while perhaps not designed to read so in fact, an ambiguous treatment of the subject makes the superficial area of the whole system appear at least three times greater than it is. And in the case of the Arkansas Geological Survey, the conclusion reached, though it made the sum of the whole, only second to that of Pennsylvania, falls short of the facts, for the reason of other discoveries made since the survey closed, which add one-fourth, if not one-third, to the total area of our Arkansas coal fields.

So has it been with everything else. But enough has been said to the reader, to understand that, if in any part of this report (already made, or which is to follow), contradiction arrays itself against either authorized or unauthorized data in their possession, evidence is not wanting to show that, at the worst, Little Rock and the state would be entitled to the benefit of a doubt.

NATIVE ZINC, COPPER, LEAD AND ANTIMONY.

Speaking from a positive standpoint, which means that the writer in the character of a "Gazette" representative, had both led and participated in discoveries

2

of zinc, lead, copper and antimony, made
in this state during the last sixteen years.

here is a delicate duty to perform which
will not be shirked now that the who e
matter seriously concerns Little Rock.

It is the question of sufficient economic
o.es in Arkansa· to maintain reduction
work at the chief city of the state, the
possibilities of which begin to loom up
along with prospective railway connections and a low-priced coal, along with
coke necessary to some processes. And
in this respect, all scientific testimony
to the con.rary, notwithstanding, the
o.es are present in quantity, particularly
the zinc, over the countie of Baxter,
Marion, Boone, Newton, and Searcy. It
occurs in the same structural form, and
to the same extent, as found in the Jop-
in and Aur r. ci-t ct- of Missou i, to
which lead the Arkansas system be onge,
but with this reservation, that in the
counties named an intersecting lead add
materially to the probabilities of the
case. It is this lat er fact which ex-
plains the wider territory over which the
zinc is distributed than seen in the Missouri zinc fields before named.

Hence, taking into account discoveries,
which time and again subs'antiated all
claim set up for the Arkansas zinc district, it does seem remarkable that no
more appreciati n is held of it at reduction centers, than if situated in the region of the Upper Amazon. The situation, true enough, is in part explained
by published statement of scientific
geologists who, under state and other
warrant for their action, have no doubt
erred in their conclusions. And the reason for saying so, is found in the fact
that practical miners have, in nearly every case of adverse decision, followed after them, only to discover bodies of zinc
ore greater than is today known on the
western continent; with a prospect held
out to others, having capital and a practical turn of mind, of striking bonanzas
in exchange for their industry and enterprise.

The mistakes, due to the scientists,
appear to have had their origin with so-
called "zinc geologists" employed by the
chief of the Arkansas Geologica Survey, to establish the economic geology
of the zinc region, but who diverted their
office to the study of North Arkansas
stratagraphy, with the usual resul', that
neither have we more information upon
the subject than was known practically
thirty years ago, nor anything added,
through such ource, to the knowledge
capitalists and mining engineers require
as a condition to their inves'ment at d
labor.

It is a long way to go about the subject,
but as related to Little Rock, by reason

of prospective connections to the Arkansas zinc fields, it had become necessary. It is known that in two instances, the mistakes of the scientists had choked off railroad enterprises through the country, not to mention an unlimited amount of capital, the investment of which in zinc properties had been arrested by the same means. As the matter stood in its uncontradicted form, it was an outrage innocently or otherwise, perpetrated upon the confidence of the public. And in the case of this report on Little Rock, it has been taken up for final disposition, with this challenge to the authors of the mistake, that if they will retrace their steps through the zinc country, and not "wabble on the gudgeon," they will in shame admit their error.

It was nothing of great moment to them, whether they hit or missed the mark. But it was much to the state of Arkansas and its capital city, as witness, the arrested development of railroads through North Arkansas. And not least of all, it was much to Little Rock, as witness for example, the possibilities the zinc and lead open up—not only in the way of reduction works upon a large scale, but in the sublimation of lead and zinc for use as paints; and which body material when added to ochre and sienna closer at hand (and to oil already pressed at this point, alone promise a great industry for Little Rock.

MANUFACTORIES NEEDED AT LITTLE ROCK.

(As conditional to material in reach.)

Cotton factories,
Woolen mills,
Oil refineries,
Soap factories,
Paint factories,
Type foundries,
Paper mills,
Starch factories,
Pottery wares,
Tripoli plants,
Tannery plants,
Car works,
Canning factories.
Boat yards,
Leather manufacturers,
Box factories,
Tobacco factories,
Match factories,
Manufacture of Alum,
Wagon factories,
Soapstone finishers,
Furniture factories,
Knit goods factories,
Coffin factories,
Manufacture of aluminum,
Carriage factories,
Manufacture of fertilizers,
Boat oar factories,
Graphite lubricators,
Pencil factories,
Stove polish manufacture,
Agricultural implement factories,
Soap stone fire brick plants,
Bucket and tub factories,
F re clay brick plants,
Granite polishing plants,
Pressed brick plants,
Brick, tile and terra cotta plants,
Crayon plants.

BOARD OF TRADE EXHIBITS.

In proceeding directly to particulars belonging to the subject of native material, upon which depends a future of manufactures, it will at least save some space in this report, if it said at once ti at exhibits collected by the Little Rock board of trade cover all facts in the case; and for this reason it will be a saving to all prospectors in time, money and anxicty, if they will give the collection, especially that of minerals, a close study, wh ch can be done at their leisure, and without any inquisitiveness on the part of others, free of cost.

It is a collection having for its e vl an exhibit of Arkansas' native material, without the intervent on of uninstructed col. ctor. and persons interested either in lands or mining properties, which makes it the only reliable display of the kind in the state, to which the public has free access. And, therefore, in passing it is only justice to say of the Little R. ck board of trade that in the public spirit exhibited by them in the matter, they are entitled to the reward it brings, now that the natural resources of the state are to turn upon efforts to start up manufactures upon a considerable scale, 1 oth for their city and state.

Exclusive of woods, textile mate. al, factory, farm, garden and orchard products, the following 's the collection nad in mind:

BOARD OF TRADE MINERAL EXHIBIT.

Semi-bitumous coal, semi-anthracite coal, zinc, lead, copper, iron, nickle, bauxite, antimony, manganese, pyrites, chalk, soapstone, novaculite, graphite, tripoli, gyp-um, talc, fire clay, tiling, slate, roofing, slate, ochre, sienna, strontia, glass sand, agate, serpentine, marble, granite, limestone, sandstone, porcelain, brown ware, yellow ware, terra cotta, pressed brick, building brick, vitrified brick, and tile clays.

ARKANSAS COAL.

While saw mills and oil mills were at the time in operation (the first conducted upon a scale and in a manner worthy of the pioneers in the industry, and the other justified in its advancement by the low price of cotton seed and the high price of oil), the subject of manufactures was not considered in connection with th's state, until the great extent of the Arkansas coal fields became known toward the close of 1886. And in this light, with other states of the south well started in the race for industrial enterprises and the money market tight ever since, the facts in the case to a considerable extent, explain the unappropriated opportunity for manufactures to which, at Little Rock and over the state, attention is called.

The presence of the coal had been prevised, first, by Prof. David Dale Owen, one of the Owen brothers of New Harmony, Ind., at the time in charge of the original geological reconnoissance of the state, and afterwards by the United States geological survey. But in both cases excepting a few well known discoveries made before their day, which are now known to have been occasioned by "faults" in the system which brought the coal to the surface, all information proceeded upon theories, the basis of which were fossil plants belonging to members of the carboniferous era. And in consequence, the writer having been instructed by the paper to determine whether coal was found in the state in quantity, it was (after six months' explotation and application to the work) left exclusively to "The Arkansas Gazette" to announce all general facts known in the premises to the present day, so exhaustively was the undertaking carried out at that time.

Of the area of the Arkansas coal field (saying nothing of a system of equal extent found to adjoin it in the Indian Territory), it is simply necessary to announce that, bringing the discoveries up to date, it is probably 2,000 square miles in extent, and occurs according to order of quantity or distribution, in the following counties reached by the Little Rock and Fort Smith, and the "Frisco" railroads, viz: Sebastian, Johnson, Faulkner, Franklin, Logan, Scott, Crawford, Pope and Yell counties. This is exclusive of any prospects allowed, now that it is becoming known, that the coal fields encroach hitherward to the immediate territory of Little Rock, with not an unreasonable hope that accident has led to a discovery of good coal within four miles of the city.

Of the quality of the coal, it should be stated in the outset, as a necessary condition to an understanding of its value, that it is a semi-bituminous, or half anthracite variety, and on that account has achieved a higher reputation as a heating agent than all other coals of a bituminous character used in maunfactures, or for making steam, excepting that of New South Wales and the Shamokin basin of Pennsylvania the fixed carbon 78 to 95 per cent being even greater, and the ash 8 to 4, even less than the coals of the two systems named. But while all this is true as to name of the coal, and therefore true as to the character of the coal, it is only true as far as it applies to coal found in Sebastian, Scott, Logan, Crawford, Franklin, Yell and Johnson counties in general.

There is a departure observed in the density of the coal, and therewith a tendency discovered to a true anthracite in the case of the Eureka m nes at Spadra in John on county, on the Little Rock and Fort Smith railroad, which quality is worked to the advantage of its owners by means of breakers. But this fact is even more emphasized the closer the present ascertained eastern limit of the coal is approached. The coal becomes harder until in Pope county its den ity. and its anthracite qualities in general as well, has for years made the product of the Onita mines, also situated on the Little Rock and Fort Smith railroad, famous over all Southwestern states. And in the case of late discoveries made in Faulkner county, wh ch is an adjoining county to the one in which Little Rock is situated, it is a dustless, dry coal, differing nothing from the Lehigh in general character excepting that it can be broken up with less cost, or, that it is not so hard and dense.

Being another discovery made by the paper, and the facts of locality reserved for this issue, it should therefore be added to the last case described that the following names of owners on whose property the coal is found, section, township and range (made public for the first time) will give the points in Faulkner county from which prospectors can work out their exploitations.

D. O. Harton, depth 60, 85 and 115 feet; section 13, township 4, range 15.

W. M. Lee, three miles from Conway, south; section 7, township 5, range 14.

Bruce place, found close to Lallow; section 8, township 5, range 14.

Crowley place, Round Mountain, situated three miles from Preston.

Beloat place, Black Fork, eighteen mile- north of Conway.

Nelso Peyton, colored, wire road, eight to nine miles from Conway.

Holland place, fifteen miles north of Conway.

J. A. Pence, corporation of Conway.

COAL STATISTICS.

Coal mined in the state for year
ended June 30, 1896, tons......889,785
Mined for year ended June 30,
1895, tons... 895,671
Number of mines worked........   39
Number of men employed....... 2,256

ARKANSAS WOODS.

In a table immediately following this division of the report, a showing is attempted of merchantable woods found in the state. The classification carried out under the respective heads of "paper stock, construction, furniture and cabinet woods," is not designed to be arbi

trary, as will no doubt suggest iself in
a glance at the varieties named. But
it is employed at this time because new
characteristics have been discovered
through an order given by the Little
Rock board of trade, for a series of exhi
bition panels now hanging on the
walls.

While no effort was made to bring out
the best color and marking of the panels
either with fillers, stains, acids, or po'-
ishing machine, remarkable, or let us say
new characteristics have developed them
selves in familiar woods found in Ark
ansas, simply by means of polishing done
by hand and a coat of varnish. And
hence, as a result of accidental discov
ery, not only is there reason for the class
ification, but it is true when said in so
many words, that the effect is one which
prac'ically adds quite a number of woods
to the 'ist commonly used in manufac
tures; the qualities, or color, marking
and strength of which (for they are all
hard woods) had evidently escaped the
notice of expert timber prospectors.

For instance: It will be found, through
the collection named, that in the willow
oak of this state manufacturers, who re
quire quarter sawed stuff, will find an
idea' wood. The omission of the wood
from the list of those used in manufac
ture, is accounted for in a number of
ways. It is in disfavor with farmers
for rail timber, and is therefore slan
dered by them. The panels exhibited
by the Little Rock board of trade, by the
state department of agriculture and man
ufacture, and by the Iron Mountain land
department, each from different parts
of the sta'e, is probably the first time an
attempt was made to give it a showing
and therefore nothing known of it in
the manufacturing wor'd. And lastly:
It is one of the most abundant oaks found
in the state; a quick grower, 50 year be
ing more than sufficient to give it a mer
chantable size; and is found growing
on "slash" lands, which makes it difficult
to "log" unless done at the dryest sea on
of the year.

A difference, in fact, will be found in
other varieties of wood named. For s
to speak, it is all round, a case in which
"local modification" appears to have
played a part as it does in geology. To
say this does not, of course, imply that
there is any wonder about the thing, but
rather, as takes place in the modifica
tion of bass wood (which is the "linden"
in the series named, and which in the
Southwest is called "linn"), it has no
pa sed wholy beyond recognition, but
it is not the same wood we know. This

much, however, is to be taken fo
granted, that the best of them will be
put to their trumps to identify without
considerable examination, any of the
Arkansas woods, excepting pine, cypress
hickory, ash and gum, which in them
selves show even more than a passing
difference. And in consequence, to take
up the reasoning where it began, much
wil be gained by hard wood prospectors
if they (those who are no! familiar wit'
the state) give either of the series of
panels described, a close study, not say
a careful experimental trial of such va
rieties as by their color and marking
show an adaptability to certain uses for
which they seek the most desirable
woods.

ARKANSAS' PAPER STOCK WOODS.

Cotton wood, sweet gum, linden, tupelo
gum, cypress.

ARKANSAS' CONSTRUCTION WOOD.

Yellow pine, white oak, hickory, pecan,
p st oak, sycamore, cypre s, cedar, as
and other oaks named under the head of
"furniture wood."

ARKANSAS' FURNITURE WOODS.

Walnut satin wood or gum, cherry,
red oak, b ack oak, wil'ow oak, cow oak
burr oak, red maple, beech and winged
elm.

ARKANSAS' CABINET AND ORNAMEN-
TAL WOODS.

Judas tree or red bud, papaw, slippery
elm, holly, sassafras, dogwood, chinque
pin, red haw, apple haw, prickly ash
shittam wood, red mulberry, bois d'arc,
river birch, sweet bay, honey 'ocust, linden and hornbeam.

TEXTILE RESOURCES.

Rather than cotton as an introduction
to the subject of textile resources, that
of wool has been substituted, for reasons
which fol ow.

The United States census report of
1890, if taken at its face value, removes
Arkansas at a single sweep from the list
of wool producing states. This is not
done arbitrarily, but it follows as a result of artificial limitations, of which it
was impossible to make notice in mere
summaries of sheep and wool produced
in th state.

For instance: The number of sheep on
farms in Arkansas aggregated only 243,
999 head. Thi does not represent the
capacity of the state for sheep raising
but when investigated, it is found to carry in it elf discouragements which yet
surround the industry in a country re
markab e for the fact that more than
five-sixths of its whole area compri es
forest lands, or open territory.

Neither does the circumstance of only 512,396 pounds of wool clipped in 1889 prove anything against the wool industry as a source of profit to the farmer. It represents instead this fact, that, together with inroads permitted upon flocks by reason of a large open territory, the producers are the victims of a conspiracy among the buyers, who have not allowed them to discover that four-fifths of the Arkansas wool, classes with the best of the South, the so-called lake wool of Louisiana.

All this is, upon investigation borne out, not only in the circumstance that only 243,999 sheep were found on 124,760 farms, and more than one-fifth of the whole number killed by dogs, during the previous year, but as still further proof of artificial instead of natural limitations take the census of improved breeds found on farms: They number only 50,460, while that of the common sheep of the country is 193,539. This has followed notwithstanding it is an industry lodged almost exclusively in the hands of white farmers, who are more thrifty in a general way than the average of Southern farmers.

Consequently, once the laws of the state are framed to protect wool growers, a ready made market for wool supplied by mills close at hand, and the light thrown upon the classification of Arkansas wool, there is no question of woolen mills doing better at Little Rock (other advantages of cheap fuel, climate, cheap labor, and price of property in included) than at any point in the South and West having 25,000 or more population.

COTTON MILLS.

As in the instance of wool, under the head of textile resources, so it is with cotton: It is doubtful whether the subject of cotton mills could be applied to local conditions without a full reasoning of the case, as follows.

However much it is our inclination to view the operation of cotton mills as local to certain states or certain parts of the Union, the proposition does not hold any better in the case of Arkansas, than it did when it was a rule with the public to contend, that, having been inaugurated by the New England States, they could not be operated successfuly in other parts of the country. This was upon the principle, that having the money, machinery and experience, it would be a doubtful experiment to erect cotton mills in other parts of the Union, especialy if, in the face of competition, eastern mills agreed upon an offensive and defensive alliance. But it was a fallacy for two reasons: First, There did not enter into the question at the time certain considerations which belong to cheaper fuel, cheaper cotton, cheaper labor, improved machinery, and more congenial conditions in general, offered by the cotton states, the natural home of the cotton mill. And second: It is to plain and practica' business reasons and not to sentiment, that we owe the general development of Southern cotton mill:, particularly in the Carolinas, Georgia and Alabama.

The same kind of fallacy was applied when a movement was discussed to remove the manufacture of boots and shoes, or at least, a corsiderab'e part of it, to St. Louis. It was contended that to do so, it would be on account of associated indu tries, practically necessary to remove eastern manufacturing towns as a whole, when in fact, it was not from any standpoint, necessary to bring former centers of such manufactures into the question. For if it was to succeed, St. Louis must look to its own intere ts, and not to that of others. This it did proceed to do by means of its home market, and by the most liberal and effective system of drumming known in the business history of the world. And almost at the close of the second year after its introduction, the spectacle was afforded of a great industry having been compelled to remove its domici'e ha'f way across the continent, not in spite of opposition found in the east, but simply by reason of tremendous business pluck and energy St. Louis brought to bear upon the undertaking.

It was something of this same spirit, though not so concentrated in form, which wrested cotton manufacture from the exclusive control of the east. And in the instance of Little Rock, and the sta'e (wi'h a large territory west f here rapidly filling up, and with Mexico, the Wes' Indies, and Central America to supply with such wares) to ucceed with cotton mil s, it will only be necessary that the right men and the opportunity meet. And this accomplished, the result witnessed in th case of the St. Louis shoe trade, will have been no more remarkable than the re-transfer, or the re-division of the cotton mill industry of the ca t and south with the southwest.

Of course, all this talk under the head of cotton mills has proceeded only upon the accepted theory of a migration of al' manufacturing industries from extreme sections of the country to the business axis of the continent (which is the Mississippi valley) accordingly as

conditions demand it. But at the same
time it has proven a strong reinforce-
ment of the question, there is no doubt
of the fact that the right man, or the
right set of men, can come here and succeed in planting larger mils and more
of them than at any point in the south
and west not fully started in the great
cotton mill race of the western continent.

They have not only the cheapest cotton of all districts given over to cotton
mills, but the be t cotton as a whole, of
al' cotton states of the Union; cheap fuel,
with good reasons for knowing that in
twelve months ime Little Rock will afford still cheaper fuel for manufactures;
cheap labor, which also includes the fact,
that it has the great "white belt" of the
state to draw from for mill operatives;
the right kind of temperature and re a-
tive humidity to compare favorably with
centers engaged in cotton manufacture;
not to add, the second smallest death
rate from consumption of all cities of
the Union. And last: A liberal and pub-
lic-spirited people who while neither able
nor willing to subscribe argely to stock
in a single industry, are yet, according
to their ability and inclination, willing
to take stock together with neighbors, in
large cotton mill enterprises, under conditions which in the outset of this report were pointed out as means to reach
the height, up to which had climbed the
cotton mill industry of certain outhern
states.

METEOROLOGICAL COMPARISON.

The fol owing table, with associated
comments was supplied by Mr. F. H.
Clarke, forecast fficial. and is intro-
duced by reasons of sugge tions made to
the writer by leading members of the
Cotton Manufacturers' Association during their visit in a body to the Atlanta
exposition.

But at the same time the data supplied
is intended to cover mete rological conditions favoring cotton manufacture, it
applies equally on the side of hea th and
climate; and therefore, by authenticated
comparison, it will be seen that Little
Rock in it natural residence conditions
differs not over much from other points
in the table.

REPORT OF LOCAL FORECAST OFFICIAL.

Mean monthly temperature and relative humidity at places named for the months of June and December, 1890 and 1895:

STATION.	Month and year	Mean temperature	Mean relative humidty. per cent. hu-
Nashua, N. H.	June, 1890	64.2	67
Lowell, Mass	June, 1890	65.3	74
Springfield, Mass	June, 1890	67.5	68
Prov dence, R. I.	June, 1890	67.7	73
Atlanta, Ga	June, 1890	78.8	70
Little Rock, Ark	June, 1890	78.2	78
Nashua, N. H.	June, 1895	68.4	70
Lowell, Mass	June, 1895	69.7	76
Springfield, Mass	June, 1895	70.7	66
Providence, R. I.	June, 1895	71.6	75
Atlanta, Ga	June, 1895	76.8	69
Little Rock, Ark	June, 1895	77.2	75
Nashua, N. H.	Dec., 1890	20.5	70
Lowell, Mass	Dec., 1890	21.9	83
Springfield, Mass	Dec., 1890	22.6	78
Providence, R. I.	Dec., 1890	28.4	66
Atlanta, Ga	Dec., 1890	45.4	75
Little Rock, Ark	Dec., 1890	45.9	75
Nashua, N. H.	Dec., 1895	29.0	75
Lowell, Mass	Dec., 1895	33.6	86
Springfield, Mass	Dec., 1895	29.0	75
Providence, R. I.	Dec., 1895	36.4	69
Atlanta, Ga	Dec., 1895	43.6	82
Little Rock, Ark	Dec., 1895	44.2	76

Of the cities above mentioned in New Hampshire, Massachusetts and Rhode Island, Nashua has 147,000 sp ndles; Lowell, 881,000; Springfield, six cotton manufacturing companies; Providence, 116,000 spindles.

The above temperature and relative humidity figures are taken from the records of the Unitde States weather bureau.

LITTLE ROCK DRINKING WATER.

(Copy.)

Hoboken, N. J., January 25, 1893.

Certificate of water analysis.

Received from Home Water Company, Little Rock, Ark.:

No 1723, Dec. 24, 1892. Sample of Arkansas R ver water, after filtering, color, none; taste, pleasant,; smell, none.

DATA OBTAINED BY ANALYSIS.

	Parts in 100,000.	Grains per gallon.
1. Free ammonia	0.0015	0.0009
2. Album noid amm nia	0.0035	0.002
3. Oxygen required to ox- diz organic matter	0.083	0.048
4. Nitrites	......	.....
5. Nitrites	0.113	0.06
6. Chlorine	0.825	0.48
7. Total hardness	5.50	3.20
8. Permanent hardness	3.50	2.04
9. Temporary hardness	2.00	1.16
10. Total solids	12.14	7.00
11. Mineral matter	10.56	6.18
12. Organic and volatile matter	1.58	0.82

(S gned.) ALBERT R. LEEDS, PH. D. Professor of Chemistry Stevens Institute of Technology.

Note—The United States gallon is taken at 58,334.95 grains.

Stevens Institute of Technology,
Hoboken, N. J., January 25, 1893.
Home Water Co., Little Rock, Ark.:

Dear Sirs—I transmit herewith the certificates of analysis of the two samples of Arkansas River water. No. 1 being the analysis of the water taken from the river before filter.ng, just as it comes to your filter plant, and No. 2 the analysis of the sample of water after it has passed through the filters.

The unfiltered water was very brown and muddy, and not suitable for domestic or manufacturing use. The filtered water was perfectly colorless, clear and brilliant, pleasant to the taste, and suited to all kinds of purposes, domestic, laundry, dyeing, bleaching, paper making, boilers, etc.

The two features in the analysis which are the most instructive are those under the head of albuminoid ammonia, and the oxygen required to oxidize organic matters. These especially indicate the quantity of fore.gn organic substances and impurities which are present. The filtered water shows a most striking and gratifying reduction. The filtered water contains only the two one-thousandth part of a grain of albuminoid ammonia. This I can assure you is unusually pure water. Yours very respectfully, (S.gned). ALBERT R. LEEDS, Professor of Chemistry Stevens' Institute of Technology.

GRANITE AND MARBLE.

So much as said having been in greater part applied to the idea of opportunites outsiders had overlooked in the ca e of Little Rock and the state, it is in consequence only true to facts in the premises to give the other side of the question, which is that of a like failure on the part of the local inhabitant to take in the situation. This oversight is in a large sense also a reason for this report. For while nothing is intended to reflect upon the inhabitants of Little Rock and the state, unless it might be argued from their preoccupation (the one with commerce, and the other with agriculture, to the exclusion of other considerations), it is yet a fact, with only a few exceptions to the rule, that what we know in detail of Arkansas' resources is due to the enterprise and public spirit of the Arkansas "Gazette."

This means all extended details, even of timber and coal, upon which turned their general development since. And therefore, leaving out antimony discovered by Von Blucher, bauxite discovered by the (Branner) Arkansas geological survey, ferro-manganese, discovered by English prospectors in search of paralusite for u e in dyeing, and lead and the sulphuret of zinc discovered by early Missouri miners (the crystalline carbonate of zinc having been discovered by "The Gazette"), there is nothing known intelligently of native material found in the state, that was not originally supplied by its representative in person, if not through the columns of the paper.

What is meant is fully illustrated in

the granite and marble found in the state. The first which extends across the country south of Little Rock, and its northern edge only one mile from the corporate limits, comprises a curved backbone ridge five miles long, with an average width exceeding two miles, and according to the vast volume of material derived from it, found as far south as the line of Louisiana, must have formed the most imposing, as it is today, the most interesting feature in the geology of Arkansas. It is an exceedingly interesting exposure particularly if we include in the bearing upon our subject the fact, that conformable to other exposures extended through several counties west of here, we have argument in it, not only of a continuous connection, but the reasonable presumption of a granite platform, so to speak, near enough to the surface not to take from the region all prospect of valuable mineral discoveries.

But, at the same time, the exposure of the granite was sufficient to set all doubts of quantity at rest, not only had the "doctors" disagreed, and in the end the system accepted as an accident due to glacial transportation, but upon the whole so indefinite were the conclusions as to deter all granite workers from its use. And in consequence, there is no instance on record where a hole ten feet deep had been sunk down upon the formation. This was up to 1887. In that year granite pavements having been adopted by Little Rock, "The Gazette" ordered an exploitation of the locality, with this result which followed, that it was at once employed for building and ornamental purposes, as well as for paving instead of Missouri granite.

Of the marble, which is found in Carroll, Boone, Baxter, Madison, Marion, Searcy and parts of Washington, Benton, Stone and Independence counties, the most accessible at the present time, is the first and last named bodies, one of which is reached at Eureka Springs and the other at Batesville, this state. Though in the fifties a block had been contributed to the Washington monument at Washington, D. C., and instantly pronounced the best contributed by our American states, it was not until 1882 that it was accepted to be a marble, the authorities before that time having hesitated to go any further with its classification than that of an "encrinital building stone," when in fact it is of the same color and grain as our so-called Tennessee marble; but with this reservation in favor of the Arkansas stone over that of Tennessee, that while it takes and retains as good polish, experiment proves that it cost fifty per cent less to prepare for market, its working qualities under the saw and chisel being that of Italian

Commercial Value of Little Rock Granite.

St. Louis, Mo., Nov. 1st., 1895.

Mr. John S. Braddock, Little Rock, Ark:

Dear Sir—We have given your material a full test in cutting and polishing and it is satisactory in every respect, and I am sure that it could be sawed as well as cut with a good gang of saws to advantage. Our red Missouri granite and the dark Quincy granite that the hardest granites in the United States; all other granites, as Barre, Maine, St. Cloud, Colorado, and California, are somewhat softer, but the Little Rock granite cuts about 25 per cent cheaper than all the above mentioned materials. No doubt if your quarry was put in proper working order and supplied with the necessary machinery, that you would be successful in getting a good market for your material. It is a good material and something new in color and formation, it stands a satisfactory crushing strength of 23,000 pounds, and takes a nice polish, and could be used for monumental as well as building work. The lowest freight rate from the East to St. Louis is 36 cents per hundred pounds in carload lots, or about 62 cents per cubic foot, and from Little Rock to our yard it would be only 7 1-2 per hundred pounds or 13 cents per cubic foot, and this difference gives us a chance to control not alone St. Louis and Missouri, but also a good many other state with your material against any Eastern granite. Yours respectfully,

WILLIAM MARTIN,
Superintendent Syenite Granite Co.

marble. The total area of the Arkansas marble district is probably 2,500 square miles.

It was designed to add in this connection something of the especial structural value of both the granite and marble, but since the report was begun, the duty has been committed to an eminent architect of this city, who is at the same time, not without the geological attainments necessary to a thorough knowledge of the subject. His paper will be found among a number which follow as a supplement to the report as a whole.

SOAPSTONE AND OCHRE.

Another thing the state has suffered in connection with its natural resources, is a species of depreciation carried on by outsiders to protect properties in kind owned or controlled by them, which, though it suggests the tricks of small minds, has its influence.

It is a form of misrepresentation which has followed so frequently, that, upon occasion inquirers writing for samples of any kind or for information, or both (if they are interested and desire notice) should be painstaking enough to show that they have a business standing at home, or at least they should afford some evidence that they mean business, elsewise, having become tired of the play they will obtain neither samples nor information. And at all events, if the necessities of the case allow it, it were better to visit Arkansas in person, and so settle the value and quantity of material at a single stroke.

The species of depreciation described has been largely directed against zinc, ochre, and soapstone. The attack on the first named has invariably issued from parties directly and indirectly interested in zinc mines. But which fact, much as it should impute their testimony, appears in general to have been overlooked.

In the case of ochre, a most extraordinary bed of which, both in body and color, is found at Monticello on the Warren branch of the Missouri Pacific railway, this state, the trick played for the last three years by St. Louis parties has been to obtain car load lots from the owners, free of cost, for trial in manufactures, the object of which was, no doubt, to stock up with a high grade ochre by means of misrepresentation, and afterwards depreciate its reputation, while they represented the washed Arkansas product as a high priced foreign importation. Something like the experience described might have occurred in connection with high colored ochre and sienna lately discovered near this city, but with the experience of others before their mind, the man who obtains any amount of it for trial or examination will have his pains for thanks, unless he can produce the documents.

A still more remarkable instance, out of many others in the same connection, was brought to light last year upon the subject of the great beds of soapstone found in this state, twenty miles west of here on the lines of railway surveys to Hot Springs, Mena, and Fort Smith. Samples were by request forwarded to parties in Vermont engaged in the preparation of soapstone finishes, with the result, that instead of coming out like men and acknowledging its value (for it has no superior on the Western continent, having been tested by manufacture into fire brick, stove lining, and bisque ware) by return mail it was learned that it was "talc," meaning talc slate, and not steatite or soapstone. And to make their attempt more ridiculous, it was discovered since, that they are palming off on the trade, under the name of soapstone finishes, etc., talc slate.

It appears from information at hand, that some questions had been raised to the effect that the strata of the soapstone is too much contorted to supply dimension material. The statement having been originated in good faith by parties prospecting the soapstone for manufacturers of furnace and stove linings, it is therefore answered in the same spirit. They did not carry their examination far enough. Three miles east of the original discovery the soapstone occurs abundantly in almost horizontal strata.

STRONTIA, MANGANESE AND COPPER.

Strontia, in abundance, is only found in the Rush creek mining district of Marion county, one of the eight counties of Arkansas that adjoin the Missouri state line. The locality is that of the crystalline carbonate of zinc found in this state, and beside strontia and zinc, is remarkable for the presence of manganese, marble, glass sands, and mammoth forest trees. The strontia, and the other material described, is found only a few miles from White river, and in the event of the beet sugar industry gaining a foothold in this state, could be delivered at all railroad crossings of White river, and at all landings on White, St. Francis, and Arkansas rivers at a small cost for transportation.

Ferro-Manganese, notwithstanding its presence in Scott and Marion counties, is found principally in two sections of the state, viz.: Independence county, which is reached over the Batesville branch of the Missouri Pacific railway, and in Polk county, which is reached over the Kansas City, Pittsburg and Gulf railroad. Though a large part of the first named district has been appropriated by Pittsburg steel companies, some of the finest manganese properties in the world remain in the hands of local parties who know its value but who are not exorbitant in their price. Throughout the second named district, which is probably the largest manganese field in the world (with brown hemalite ore, coal and lime not far away), desirable properties were some years ago covered by options in the interest of Memphis capitalists. These options have no doubt expired long ago, and at a venture one would be free to say that the opportunity is in greater part open to investors.

Copper is found in the Tomahawk valley of Searcy county, situated immediately south of Marion county. It occurs in both a carbonate and oxide form; and taken in connection with its proximity to mineral discoveries made in Marion, Boone and Newton counties, and in the neighboring valley of St. Joe (with nothing thoroughly explored of the country lying between) is in itself a departure from a rule which promises good results if the oppotunity is improved by careful exploitation. Being otherwise surrounded, by a good farm and fruit region, it is not unappreciated, but remains an arrested development because its value is depended upon railway construction through the country from Harrison to Little Rock. And upon the first signal of such construction which is not impossible at this time, it can be expected to come widely into notice.

ANTIMONY AND GYPSUM.

Antimony occurs in Polk county in that part which immediately adjoins the counties of Howard and Sevier, all three of which are threaded by the Kansas City, Pittsburg and Gulf railroad. Much, if not the greater part of the territory where found, was a few years ago owned by the United States Antimony company, of Philadelphia, who erected a reverberating furnace, sunk shafts, and prepared to reduce the ore. But upon the occasion of a visit made to the plant in 1888, it was learned that the cost of wagon transportation to distant railway points rendered further operations impracticable, or at least too costly; since which time no further developments have been made. It is presumed that the same company owns the property, and therefore is not upon the market. But in the event of others wishing to share in the antimony discoveries, Lieut. Van Blucher should be sought out through the officers of the Kansas City, Pittsburg and Gulf railroad. He is the discoverer, and is, upon good authority, known to have most desirable antimony properties in hiding.

3

Gypsum is found in Pike county, and forms the base of conspicuous headland flanking a stream known as the Little Missouri river, a confluence of the famous Ouachita river. The nearest approach by rail is over the Prescott and Wallace burg connection of the Missouri Pacific, and over the Nashville branch of the Missouri Pacific. In connection with county where found it should be added that the Smithton and Pike City connection of the Missouri Pacific railway penetrates a region of Pike county, affording the purest porcelain clay found in the state, notwithstanding Arkansas is probably richer in plastic clay, and Little Rock the center of a greater variety of merchantable clays, than found elsewhere in the Union. And in connection with the subject of clays applied directly to pottery uses, it will be found treated in an exhaustive manner by Prof. Thomas, of Alexander, this state, in an article from his pen, which, as one of a series, supplements this report.

HARDWOOD AND PINE DISTRICTS.

It was originally designed to supply at a glance, by shadings, on a map prepared for the purpose, the localities of prevailing hardwood and pine forests in the state. This design was abandoned, and the accompanying large map to the report substituted for the reason that the reduced size of the maps ordered, defeated the end for which they were intended.

Though a stranger to the state, readers who apply the designations which follow will obtain an equally satisfactory notion of the prevailing timbers throughout the state; remembering, of course, that in the case of streams traversing pine counties, there is no exception to the rule of hardwood timber immediately flanking their course.

The hardwood district of Arkansas comprises conspicuously, Northern and Eastern Arkansas; and in this state by the term Eastern Arkansas is meant that part of the state lying east of White river as far south as the Arkansas; and Northern Arkansas that part of the state lying north of the Arkansas and west of White river. The exception in the case of both Northern and Western Arkansas comprises Cleburne, Van Buren, Stone, Izard, Randolph and Clay, which are pine counties, with fractional areas of pine found in counties included under the head of hardwood counties.

The pine district of the state is notably Southern and Western Arkansas. The first comprises all territory of the state lying south of the Arkansas river and south of the southern half of the Arkansas division of Missouri Pacific railway. The second comprises territory lying west of Little Rock, south of the Arkansas river, and north of the southern half of the Arkansas division of the Missouri Pacific railway. The exceptions to the rule in the case of South Arkansas are Chicot, Desha and Lincoln counties; and the exceptions in the case of Western Arkansas are Sebastian, Logan and Franklin counties, which are hardwood districts.

OUTPUT OF WOOD PLANTS.

When arriving at the subject of timber resources in another part of this report, it was decided to omit the annual output of wood plants operated in this state. The subject appeared to be surrounded with too many obstacles to success, and upon the whole, the last two years had not been advantageous to the saw-mill industry, and to wood plants in general. But since the first of the year other means of a reliable character, having been supplied to the writer, the following will be found, within a few thousand feet, to be the average of the last three years.

The information as supplied has been for satisfactory reasons divided, into saw-mill and miscellaneous wood products. The following is the table of plants according to classification of owners, or according to product for which they claim a specialty. The total number of plants included, all of them situated on railroad lines, is 467:

OUTPUT OF SAW MILLS.

Yellow Pine	492,827,000
Oak f all kinds	93,746,000
Oak and pine	94,474,000
Oak and cypress	27,035,000
Cypress and pine	32,200,000
Cypress lumber	29,200,000
Oak, gum and cottonwood	35,000,000
Oak, hickory and gum	39,200,000
Oak, gum and cypress	24,100,000
Oak and poplar	25,000,000
Oak and gum	16,000,000
Oak, ash and gum	6,900,000
Oak, walnut and elm	3,050,000
Oak, walnut and pine	3,000,000
Oak, p ne and cypress	3,000,000
Oak, hickory and sycamore	2,500,000
Miscellaneous lumber	45,000,000

OUTPUT MISCELLANEOUS WOOD PRODUCTS.

	Carloads.
Staves	320
Staves and heading	722
Tight barrel staves	206
Bucker staves	47
Staves and hoops	38
Staves and barrels	51
Shaped hoops	32
Heading	27
Cottonwood box material	37
Miscellaneous	231

Wagon material, feet	2,231,000
Hickory slabs, feet	1,800,000
Cypress staves	7,210,000
Cypress shingles	181,675,000

LOCAL MANUFACTURES.

While all details of this report on local conditions have been focussed upon
propspects Little Rock offers to manufactures of many kinds, the reason of the
case is not altogether on one side of the
question, when it is asked: What has
been done in the way of industrial enterprises, or manufactures?

The answer is this: To use no data
originating at Little Rock or in the state,
a reply is found a way back in the census
reports of 1890, which, while much improved since then, covers the case sufficiently to prove, that when accommo-
dated to the situation at the time, enough
money had been forthcoming to show
that all her people were not indifferent
to manufactures.

For example, notwithstanding outside
of the city and county, Arkan as in gen-
era was backed in the race by hundreds
of saw mills, and Fort Smith, Pine Bluff,
Texarkana, Helena, Camden, Newport,
and other points in common, not without
entries for industrial honors, out of a
total investment of $14,971,614, in dif-
ferent kinds of industries, named under
the head of manufactures, Little Rock
and the county in which it is situated,
supplied little less than one-fifth of the
total amount so invested throughout the
state.

The sum has been increased, or
nearly doubled since then, there
having been nothing overdrawn in the
census report, nor in fact, full justice
done to the matter, which is admitted in
foot notes to the recapitulation pub lshed
under the authority of the government.
But the facts of the case are equal to
all rea onable demand manufacturing
investors might make, as a "show down,"
preliminary to planting their money in
the city.

It is a showing that is particularly grat-
ifying since it brings to ight the cir-
cumstance, that the cost of a product
valued at $100, is less in Arkansas than
in the following forty states and terri-
tories of the Union, viz.: Maine, New
Hampshire. Vermont. Massachusetts,
Rhode Island, Connecticut, New York,
New Jersey, Pennsylvania. Delaware,
Virginia, West Virginia, South Carolina,
Georgia, Florida, Alabama, Mississippi,
Louisiana, Tenne see, Kentucky, Mis
souri, Indian Territ ry. New Mexico,
California, Oregon, Montana, Nevada,
Nebraska, Kansas, Scuth Dakota, North
Dakota, Minnesota, Michigan, Iowa, Illi-
nois, Indiana, Ohio and Wyoming.

In connection with the table of sum-

maries of manufactures which follow. it
should be said that the summaries of
"Little Rock Manufactures" do not include items and figures that applied at
the time to suburban districts. This fact,
in consequence, qualifies the table of
"Little Rock and County" to a considerable degree, the outlying districts,
which were the seat of many industrial
plants, having been the next year added
to the city. The outcome is, that the
table on "Little Rock and County" represents, if not wholy, at least in the greatest part, industries which, at the time
represented, in fact, Little Rock manufactures

It should be explained in the same connection that the term "total capital invested" used in the tables, includes the
value or cost of lands, buildings, machinery, implements and tools.

And, to come nearer home: Take the
table of "Manufactures, Little Rock and
County," and if traced back through details for which it comprises the aggregated sums of each, interesting discoveries will be made by those who had not
looked at the question seriously. For in
stance: Take the following items and
compare them with facts which parallel
the case on the side of commerce in Lit
tle Rock. viz.: Number of establishments,
151; number of employes, 2279; invested
in plants, $4,145,299; distributed as cost
of material , total wages paid, and mis
ce laneous expenses, $3,455,927.

MANUFACTURES, LITTLE ROCK AND COUNTY, CENSUS OF 1890.

Number of employes	2,279
Total capital invested	$2,852,403
Invested in plants	$1,872,468
Live assets	979,935
	$2,852,403
Number of establishments	151
Total value of products	$4,145,299
Cost of materials	$1,918,998
Total wages paid	1,267,503
Miscellaneous expenses	269,426
	$3,455,927

LITTLE ROCK MANUFACTURES.

Number of employes	1,534
Total capital invested	$2,677,955
Invested in plants	$1,807,201
Live assets	870,745
	$2,677,955
Number of establishments	124
Value of products	$3,120,677
Cost of materials	$1,396,773
Total wages paid	830,857
Miscellaneous expenses	254,227
	$2,481,857

ARKANSAS MANUFACTURES.

Number of employes	15,972
Total capital invested	$14,971,614

Invested in plants	$10,448,236
Live assets	4,523,378
	$14,971,614
Number of establishments	2,073
Value of products	$22,659,179
Cost of materials	$12,397,261
Total wages paid	5,749,888
Miscellaneous expenses	1,035,256
	$19,182,405

LITTLE ROCK MANUFACTURES.

(Dun's local Agency Census, 1896.)

Cotton seed oil mills	4
Cotton delinter plants	1
Foundry and machine shops	5
Engines and boilers	3
Railway car shops	2
Street railway car shops	1
Wagons and carriages	4
Cotton gin factories	1
Furniture factories	3
Planing mills	8
Sash, doors and blinds	4
Wooden pulleys	1
Saw mills	4
Tobacco ad cigar factories	5
Candy factores	2
Confectioners	3
Bread and cakes	14
Electric light plants	5
Architectural iron works	3
Manufacturing druggists	12
Saddlery and harness	5
Boot makers	25
Woman's clothing	24
Tailors' custom work	19
Coffins and burial cases	4
Painting and paper hanging	15
Printing and publishng	11
Blacksmiths and farriers	23
Photographers	6
Manufacturng jewelers	2
Baking and yeast powders	2
Tents and sails	2
House builders	40
Cotton compresses	3
Dyeing and cleaning	3
Illuminating and heating gas	1
Hand stamps	1
Artificial ice	3
Lock and gunsmithing	5
Marble and stone works	4
Bicycle and repair shops	9
Mineral and soda waters	5
Lime and cement	1
Granite quarries	6
Brick manufacturers	4
Plumbing and gas fitting	4
Roofing and roofing material	6
Saw repairs and grinding	3
Tinners and coppersmiths	6
Vinegar and cider factories	2
Trunk factories	2
Mattress factories	4
Plastering and stucco works................	7
Flouring and corn mills	2
Staves and wholesale staves	7
Cocperage plants	3
Mechanical dentists	12
Broom and brush factories	2
Boxes, fancy and paper	1
Boxes, wooden	2
Brass foundres	3
Shirt factories ....,..........	2
Sewing machine repairing	3
Handle factories	1
Wine covering	1
Upholstering	4
Cornice makers	4
Wrought iron works	1
Fence and wre factories	1
Woodenware manufacture	1
Total	401

SOCIAL CONDITIONS OF LITTLE ROCK.

Of social conditions: It is only fair to the question of Little Rock's social fabric, to say that it is neither too rigid and erect in outline to fit well into the wider environments of the west, nor too complex, not to suggest something of refined conceptions and to tes. And if this is true, embarrassing as it may be to those of us who criticise western communities (not for what we know of them, but by reason of locality and surroundings), is it not possible, that, because of the standpoint from which we look, they have the advantage of us, being never too dull of wit to know at sight, a hyper critical observer?

It is at 'east certain, that we never get at the best side of western life, if it 's only looked at from the exterior. There is a certain openness in manner and speech, and a certain regard for comfort and economy in dress, behind which, if we look closely, there are faces which always look out kindly upon humanity And what is a better test of the morals and intelligence of a man or woman than a consciousness of the truth, that the whole world is kin?

Consequently with this much understood, not only is it easy to get at the fact of Little Rock's society, but also the conditions of life from which it is recruited. It does not in any respect compare unfavorably on the surface with the best of our American cities. But it is more than is implied by its well-dressed members and its charming homes. And, therefore, however other cities of the Southwest claim greater wealth, they cannot, as a rule, show better men and women in their social ranks than those of Little Rock.

In the last sentence we have, in fact, the application of the subject to the ground taken for Little Rock: of being, in all seriousness, the only one of many cities visited in the United States where (wanting in nothing that is derived from money, blood, travel, fashion, and education), social conditions are, in the best and widest senses, favorable to mill owner and mill worker. What is meant is simply this: If upright and industrious, the worker of any kind will find here more good people of his class, who have come from farms and not from slums, than any city of its size in the Union; and the mill owner, if a gentleman, will in a short time receive a kinder and completer recognition, according to his social qualities and ambitions,

than men of ten and twenty times their
capital have received all their lives
from cities where they live.

It is an exclusive people to those whose
character or qualities do not fit them to
wear well out of their sphere, whether
of business or morals, but never more
generous hosts and neighbors than when
their hospitality and friendship are put
to the touch by the right men and wo
men. It is, moreover, not an exclusive
ly Southern people, but from all parts
of the Union, which, in part, no doubt,
accounts for the bearing marking them
above all people of the Southwest. For
rather than noisy, or too free and easy,
they are, in general, reserved and self
possessed, beyond those of Memphis, St
Louis, Kansas City, Dallas, Houston,
Galveston and San Antonio. And it is
no doubt in consequence of this char-
acteristic that they escape special notice,
when others, more forward, strut out a
welcomed recognition, before the stran
er could take their soundings. But
their reserve has its advantages, as wit
ness their sons and daughters who have
gone out to more stations of honor and
trust, and to more refined and stately
homes in other cities and states, than in
proportion to number of inhabitants, has
followed class for class, in the last twen
ty years history of Southern cities, ex
cepting Baltimore, Richmond, Charles
ton, Louisville, Memphis and New Or
leans.

COMMERCE OF LITTLE ROCK.

Though this report is, in the main
given over to the subject of manufactures, and the reasonings of Little Rock's
commerce held back, it is far from the
truth to imply, from the circumstances,
that it is not now holding its own, or
that it will not hold is own hereafter. It
has its limitations, it is true, but they are
limitations which do not apply in the case
of its retail trade, however, agriculture
and the lumber industry of the state are
unequal to the demands, not to say, rea
sonable necessities of Arkansas' rapidly
growing population.

Any difficulties in the way only apply
to the jobbing trade, which (by reason of
restrictions necessitated at the hands of
railroads, and a consequent competition
of St. Louis, Memphis, New Orleans, and
Kansas City, in this state) is to some extent an "arrested development," but
which, under late pressure brought to
bear upon the situation, will no doubt
disappear; and in consequence the wholesale dealer re-appear in its trade in num
bers called for by Little Rock's opportunity and its irresistible growth.

An important reason which has influenced the condition of Little Rock's wholesale trade, complained of, will be found in changes made in the purchase of cotton, formerly consigned to cotton factors at New Orleans, Memphis, and St. Louis, but now in general bought at first hand from producers, or from merchants doing business at points nearest to the producer. It was a form of business countenanced by precedents of the cotton trade, but which in passing away now completely unmasks the element of danger there was involved in it for legitimate business men. And as a result, having been wholly or generally abated only during the past few years, and freight rate limitations, within the state, not attacked upon general principles, it remains for Little Rock to improve the opportunity.

It also follows in the same connection, that with the double star of commerce and manufacture to sail by, and plenty of sea room to "tack" in, during periods of adverse winds, not all of Little Rock is seen, if it is judged by limitations, which to break up, as now understood, only needs a strong pull, a long pull, and a pull all together on the part of her people.

Regarding the retail side of the question: We have in it, at a glance, an argument which at the same time it is a credit to Little Rock, is also a pointer to means through which it is practicable to build a wholesale trade equal to the demands of its own territory, if not absolutely the whole demands of the state. Like its metropolitan contemporaries, you can not only obtain in the city at first hand, every thing running up from a hay stack to a steam engine, but in its place as the social center of the state, it is the only absolute center of fashion found in Arkansas. And accordingly, while not a hand is turned against other points of trade in the state, it has been, with good reason for congratulations, the determination of its merchants, not to sacrifice the advantage it perpetuates, either to greed, or to its twin evil of commerce, shoddy; with this result, that its retail trade doubles itself during the year because of patronage which, until a few years back, had been bestowed upon New York, Chicago, St. Louis and Memphis and the ranks of local patrons increased more than fifty per cent by citizens in general of Arkansas, and of adjoining territory.

LITTLE ROCK COMMERCIAL PLANTS.

(Dun's Local Agency Census, 1896.)

Wholesale dry goods and clothing	3
Wholesale hats, caps and millinery	1
Wholesale boots and shoes	1
Wholesale and retail India rubber goods	1
Wholesale hardware	2

42

INHABITANTS OF LITTLE ROCK.

Being for several reasons a matter of
general comment, it is hardly necessary
to say, that in approaching the subject of
Little Rock's "inhabitants," and therefore by implication, the subject of Arkansas' population, one is reminded of
the "Cockney," who, as answer to an inquiry why water was sprinkled on white
cloth to bleach it when exposed to the
sun, was informed that it did good by
reason of offices the water performed in
passing through the cloth.

It is not contended, excepting in extreme cases, that any one seriously believed the story of the "Arkansaw Traveler," but there is no doubt that its offices, as it ran through the public mind, did the state no good. To this day, let the reputable citizen of the state go abroad, and it is the rule and not the exception, if he does not attract attention, insantly it is announced that he is from Arkansas. But meanwhile this takes place, little thought is given to the fact, that however the story may be predicated upon a frontier civilization, as it was conceived fifty years ago, it holds no more in these latter days, than would the "witch burning" civilization of the New England states apply to descendants of those people, not to mention an application of the "pipe and gin" civilization to the Knickerbocker descendants of New York, or the "Sucker" civilization of Illinois, or the "broncho" civilization of Texas.

There was an end to it all sometime in their history, and why not in the case of Arkansas? One thing is certain, if others can stand it, and not afterwards blush for their intrepidity in reaching conclusions, the Arkansan can, especially since the matter will in the end take care of itself. And in the case of Little Rock, there is not an inhabitant of adult years, who, in the face of authenticated reports of the government (not to add current assurance of the day) does not know, that the hypercriticism of himself and neighbors is founded either upon ignorance, prejudice, or malice. This is upon general principles.

If on the other hand we predicate the matter upon origin of inhabitants, and admit the hypothesis, that their standard of civilization is not up to the measure of the critics, it will be found that the inequality is not altogether native to the state. But this is parleying with the question, when, despite the "mistakes of Moses," it is a fact, that from the highest to the lowest, society at Little Rock, and throughout Arkansas, is permeated by less rottenness than any city or state of the Union, and to the proof of which any one who is interested, is challenged to consult the authenticated reports of the government upon all subjects entering into the question, whether of morals, education, business, or politics.

Of the origin of Little Rock's inhabitants: Take the tables which follow, extracted from the census of 1890, and upon the ground that the exposition applies almost wholly to adult persons, it will be found that the injustice done the state, in the case of its capital city, is re-

buked in the fact of a general if not cos
mopolitan origin of its inhabitants.

Before passing from the subject it
should be added, that the number of inhabitants credited to Little Rock in the
census of 1890, 25,874, is correct as far
as it goes. But it does not go far enough.
The annexation of suburban districts, al-
lnded to under the head of manufactures,
in the case of population, included ad-
ditions to the city which, for the purpose of avoiding city taxation, had not
been included in the census of either
1870, 1880, or 1890, and growing out of
which omission, Little Rock will, in effect, show in 1900, the largest gain of
population in ten years, of all cities of
the southwest having more than 25,000
inhabitants. Judging alike from the di-
rectory, school, and franchise census of
the city, it can be safely assumed (short
of an house to house census) that the
inhabitants of Little Rock, rather than
less, number more than 40,000.

NATIVE WHITE POPULATION OF LIT-
TLE ROCK.

(United States Census of 1890.)

Oh.o	159	Tennessee	1,836
Illinois	126	Mississippi	1,123
New York	121	Alabama	772
Missouri	168	Kentucky	642
Indiana	82	Texas	449
Kansas	71	Louisiana	229
Pennsylvania	59	Indian Ter.itory.	28
Michigan	40	Califcrnia	16
Iowa	34	Maryland	15
Nebraska	30	Georgia	16
Wisconsin	18	South Caro.ina	13
Massachusetts	15	Colorado	8
Minnesota	8	Virginia	9
Rhode Island	5	New Mex co	5
Maine	4	Oregon	4
Connect cut	4	Utah	3
New Hampshire.	3	North Carolina..	4
Vermont	1	West Virg.nia	3
New Jersey	8	Florida	3
Nevada	2	Delaware	1
Alaska	2	Washing.on	1

Total native whites, not born in Arkansas 6,143
Total white, natives of Arkansas.... 7,849

Grand tota: of whites, natives 13,992

FOREIGN POPULATION OF LITTLE
ROCK.

(United States Census of 1890.)

Germany	1,087	Denmark	9
Ireland	247	Norway	9
England	205	Bohemia	9
Canada	132	Hungary	7
Switzerland	53	Austral a	4
Sweden	56	Wales	4
France	49	Africa	2
Scotland	44	West Ind.es	2
Italy	44	India	1
Austria	31	Greece	1
Poland	28	Belgium	1
Russia	17	Scuth America	1
China	15	Mexico	1
Holland	10	Not specified	51

SUMMARIES OF LITTLE ROCK'S POPU-
LATION.

(United States Census of 1890.)

Total population 1890 25,874
Total foreign population 2,122

Total native population 23,752

```
Total natives of Arkansas ..............11,052
Natives not born in Arkansas ........12,700
Total white population 1890.............16,114
Negroes, including 21 Chinese, etc .... 9,760

Excess of white population ........... 6,354

Total families in Little Rock 1890........5,496
Total dwellings in Little Rock, 1890......4,980

Excess of families to total dwellings .. 516

Total male population, 1890 .............12,962
Total female population, 1890 ...........12,912

Excess of males to total females ...... 50
```

STATUS OF SCHOOLS AND CHURCHES.

As called for in efforts designed to propitiate manufactures, and therefore convey a clear idea of existing conditions favoring the welfare and comfort of those invited to share its fortunes, it would be difficult to round off any serious report of Little Rock, without applying the school and church tests which mark the history of our American civilization.

Taken at their face value, there is no difference from what is observed at other points where the family is built up and protected upon lines of defense dictated by reason and common sense. Nor in fact is it necessary to go elsewhere for illustration of views expressed upon the subject by continental writers who had visited the United States, the substance of which is as follows: That given the premises of native inhabitants, of respectable parentage, and their age over twenty-five years, there is no doubt of a noble likeness running through the character and sentiments of our people, traceable directly to the free school and free church system of our people; and therefore, that while in the truest sense creditable to the genius of our institutions, they have been, are now, and always will be, the basis of greater stability upon which rests our free government, than all the Republics known in the world's history.

But at the same time all this is admitted, and the dictum, set forth, accepted as a splendid tribute to our school and church system, why is it at variance with that which, in common, has been accepted of this state, and therefore by implication, accepted of its capital city?

It is true, that at a venture, but few of us can acquit ourselves of the charge upon other grounds than thoughtlessness or prejudice. And yet, it does not mitigate the effect, if we only admit the mistake without repairing the damage. It is not, that the arrow sped from the bow is lost, but it is the careless and indifferent view held of the consequence, when in all fairness and justice as much, if not more diligence should be displayed

to repair wrong, as we would in the case
of a person whom, upon first acquaintance, we had misunderstood, or whom
we had misjudged or slandered to our
friends.. The failure to do so is, therefore, in the same sense an injustice,
whether we care to think so or not.

Beyond this, it is not necessary to go
with the subject than the fact, that in the
highest sense so intent are the people of
Little Rock upon an advanced plane for
their church and school, that at a venture, it were not too much to declare
their offices surpassed in no city of the
world. They are not all saints, not by a
good deal. Nor have they and their
children become be-spectacled from por-
ing over ponderous tomes. But they
comprise in greater part the best type of
Southern, Eastern and Western people it
is possible to find intimately associated
under the roof-tree of any city in the
world; who, at the same time they fear
God and hate the devil, show forth a
composite character plainly derived from
Puritan, Cavalier and Hugenot, which
means that their mental and moral life
may be expected to keep pace with the
business sagacity, excellences, and graces
of the three types named.

In the tables which follow it was not
deemed necessary to go beyond summaries supplied by the local superintendent of public instruction. They expres-
at a glance all force it is possible to use
in a discussion of public school matters
in our Southwestern country. Nor was it
thought necessary to go beyond a mere
summary of means Little Rock otherwise supplies under the heads of colleges, kindergarten, and studios. It is
sufficient from the number given to
know that they are demanded by the city
and state.

LITTLE ROCK PUBLIC SCHOOLS.

(Data based upon yearly averages for ten
years.)

Average enrollment of whites 2,659
Average enrollment of negroes 1,704

Total average yearly enrollment 4,363

Average attendance of whites 1,990
Average attendance of negroes 1,114

3,104

Number of teachers employed for whites..40
Number of teachers employed for ne-
groes 21

Total average teachers employed 61

Average high school graduates, white....19
Average high school graduates, negroes..10

Total average of high school graduates..29

Average cost of supervision and instruction $35,979 77
Average total expendiutre $58,800 83
Grand total expenditures for ten
years $588,008 30

LITTLE ROCK PUBLIC SCHOOLS.
(Operations of the present year.)

Number of teachers employed 84
Number of pupils enrolled, 1896.........5,118

Total cost for instruction ....$ 45,506
Total cost for all purposes 73,712
Total value of property 313,103

CHURCHES, SCHOOLS, SCHOOLS OF IN-STRUCTION, ETC.

(Arkansas Gazette Census, 1896.)

Churches of all denominations 52
Y. M. C. A. rooms and library 1
Young men's institute and library, Catho-
lic 1

Public schools 9
Colleges and academies 5
Parochial schools 3
Kindergarten 7

Medical college 1
Law school 1
Business colleges 2
Art studios 3
Mus cal studios, vocal 8
Musical studios, instrumental 13
Piano instructors 173
Pipe organ instructors 3
Dancing school instructors 2

LITTLE ROCK WATER SERVICE.

Pressure to the square inch, 75 to 80 pounds
Distributing mains, 4 to 20 inches, 50 miles.
Double muzzle fire hydrants, 320.
Diameter of standpipe, 20 feet; height, 150 feet.
Reservoir capacity, 11,000,000 gallons.
Pumping capacity, 14,000,000 gallons.
Probable cost of plant, $600,000.
As part of th s equipment they use a 6,000,000 capacity Worthingt n high duty engine.

PUBLIC COMFORT IN GENERAL.

Cost of sewer system ....$ 30,000
Fire apparatus and alarm system.. 34,000
Cost of telephone plants............. 175,000
Water works—probable cost 600,000
Gas and electric light plants 750,400
Cost of street railways 1,250,000

Total cost $2,849,400

HAT BAND SUMMARY.
(City of Little Rock.)

Area of city in square miles........ 11
Number of inhabitants 40,000

Value of Church property ....$ 891,000
Public buildings, State and city...... 2,448,000

Total value $3,339,000

Number of manufacturing plants.. 401
Number of commercial plants 706
Banks, agencies, lawyers, doctors,
etc.......... 319

Total number 1,426

Manufacturing capital employed....$5,156,000
Other incorporated plants 1,452,000
Banking capital 1,253,000

Total, not including commerce
in general $7,851,000

Value of manufactured products
1896 ....$ 8,190,000
Trade sales for year 1896 16,612,421
Total miscellaneous transactions .. 7,310,070

Total, exclusive of banking.....$32,112,697

LITTLE ROCK BOARD OF TRADE.

In clo-ing this report it is due to say
of the Little Rock Board of Trade that
no body of business men realize more
fully the opportunities of their city and
state, and to that end have entered the
race of progress and development in a
spirit worthy of men who, knowing the
right way to success, have the courage
to follow it, notwithstanding discouragements that beset them at the start.

Rather than an affair that is attended
to at the leisure of its members, it is a
working body which in its parts represents the strongest men found in the
state, and therefore with a view to util-
izing each one's ability and influence to
the best advantage, its membership is divided into three classes. Those whose
province it is to advance and defend the
city as a whole, and therefore not only
set the battle of commercial and industrial development in array, but plan for
it. The second clas- comprises the rank
and file who are always in the saddle.
The th rd clas: is composed of the re-
serves who are drawn upon the supply
vacancies in the ranks of the first two
mentioned; and all three at all times re-
sponding to the call of duty promptly as
the general alarm is sounded.

But the principal advantage it proves
to Little Rock is the fact that from its
zeal and liberality it is at all times possible to evolve a personal and general co-
operation that is more than money when
there is need to promote new
enterpri.es—a bright-faced, open-
armed, welcome, behind which
Little Rock stands pledged with
its manhood and womanhood to do
justice to the man or woman who has a
right to personal as well as business recognition. And for this reason alone, saying nothing of a readiness to do the best
possible for those needing help to get desirable industries on their feet, there is
not another body of organized business
men like it today in America.

As expressed in the body of the report,
on the nativity of its citizens in general,
it is also a remarkable body in the sense
that it includes most reputable people
from all parts of the Union, which fact
probably accounts for the readiness with
which they receive others of equally reputable personal and busine-s standing,
instantly that occasion demands action
along lines laid down for their government. But even with this admission, the
gist of the thing rema ns when it i re-
flected that, however the origin of population in other cities compares with Little Rock, none of them compare with it
in the cordiality of their greeting, without wa ting to see "how much there is
in it" for the individual. And in conse-

quence, acting upon the principle that a gentleman and lady, is a gentleman and lady in Little Rock as they are at home, it is no wonder that, having tasted of its confidence in others as in her own citizenship, those who have need to change their domicile never fail to return.

As an incorporated institution it should perhaps be added of the Little Rock Board of Trade that, dating from last fall, it is in fact a consolidation of a senior and junior body of business men, and is therefore the only body of the city to be approached by outsiders upon any subject requiring general action and encouragement, as well as information of all kinds whether of railroads, industries, native material, or public improvements of any kind.

OFFICERS LITTLE ROCK BOARD OF TRADE.

President—W. W. Dickinson, wholesale and retail hardware.

Vice President—Henry M. Cooper, Little Rock Cooperage Company.

Treasurer—John G. Fletcher, German National Bank.

Secretary—George G. Harkness.

DIRECTORS LITTIE ROCK BOARD OF TRADE.

John W. Pope, cotton factor, Howell Cotton Company.

T. H. Jones, commission merchant.

J. A. Fones, wholesale and retail hardware.

Joh F. Boyle, fire insurance.

J. W. Blackwood, attorney at law.

Chas. S. Stifft, wholesale and retail jeweler.

J. H McCarthy, capitalist and contractor.

H. P. Edmonson, retail grocer.

F. B. T. Hollenberg, Hollenberg Music Company.

W. S. Mitchell, Arkansas Democrat Company.

M. L. DE MALHER.

THE MERCANTILE AGENCY
R. G. DUN & CO.

Little Rock, Ark., Jan. 6, 1897.
Col. M. L. DeMalber, City:

Replying to yours of recent date will say my conclusions upon the questions laid before me, are as fol ows:

The year 1896, which has just closed, has been full of many perplexities for merchants, manufacturers, etc., and as a rule trade for the year just ending has not been satisfactory, yet this has been the case throughout the country; and while we have felt the general depression, yet we are in no worse condition than many other trade centers. The fall and winter trade in jobbing lines ha averaged fair, but the retail trade has not been up to expectation and the very unsatisfactory results of late are largely attributed to local causes, for instance—short crops, low-priced cotton, etc., which has made money scarce with the masses; besides the hard times that the country has been passing through has caused the consumer to be more economical, and both traders and consumers have been more economical and bought in the main for actual needs or demands; this conservation has, in a great measure, assisted to curtail the usual volume of trade.

Yet as a jobbing market, Little Rock is holding her own and in comparison to other markets of the same size is gaining in importance gradually every year. It is true there are not as many jobbing houses in the city as we had a few years ago, but this is the case also with many other markets and is accounted for by the depreciation in values which has made profits small; at the same time the expenditure necessary to operate a who'esale business has not practically lessened in comparison to the small profits realized; therefore, those who have capital are timid, the results being uncertain, and do not care t vest in large enterprises, especially since the country has been in a state of suspense from an epidemic of failures.

The jobbing merchants of Little Rock who are now in business are progressive and enterprising; they cover a greater territory and have more traveling salesmen than heretofore. Ten years ago the trade of this city was principaly confined to a radius of 125 miles. Now her merchants are seeking trade throughout the entire State of Arkansas, North Louisiana, the Indian Territory and some of her merchants have considerable trade even in Texas.

As to her manufacturing interest will say, with a few exceptions, no progress

has been made during the past year,
which has resulted from the low price of
products and small margins. The manufacturing of cotton oil, which is a large
industry here, has been to some extent
handicapped by the low price of their
product and the results have not been
all that could be wished for. The lumber manufacturers have to a greater
extent felt the depression, the hard
times having been felt throughout the
whole country, which curtailed building and improvements, thus making the
demand for lumber only moderate and
low prices have prevailed. To the
lumber dealers 1896 has been the most
unsatisfactory for years, yet the outlook
in this branch of manufacturies seems
more hopeful and a good trade is antic-
ipated during the coming spring.

During the year just ended the Little
Rock cotton mills was forced to shut
down, leaving creditors unprovided for.
This mill, up to the time of its closing,
turned out large amounts of cotton
yarn, twine, etc. The low prices had
some effect upon it; yet the prime cause
of its failure to sustain itself was largely on account of the plant having bee
bought principally on credit. The op-
erator, therefore, relied mainly upon outside assistance to run it. The mill in
1895, even under these conditions, did
very well, but during the early part of
1896 was compelled to manufacture on
a delcining market which handicapped
it to such an extent that it was forced
to close. There seems to be no doubt
but that this plant could be made an ul-
timate successs with sufficient capital
to operate it, for it is one of the best
equipped mills for its size in the southwest.

Some of the factories engaged in the
manufacturing of fixtures, sash, doors,
architectural woodwork, are not sati -
fied with the result of the year, while
others who are engaged in the same line
state they did not make much money,
but express themselves as being fairly
well satisfied considering the year which
they had to contend with.

One of the argest and most succes -
ful plants located here and in fact on
of the best plants in this section is engaged in manufacturing cotton presses,
cot on seed machinery, iron workes,
etc. This enterprise ha· done a large
and profitable business and their prod
uct is shipped to every cotton-produ
ing country in the world, and has a
large domestic and foreign trade, ship-
ping a large amount of their output to
Mexico and Europe, and it is a paying
ins itution and one that this city and
state can be proud of.

Another of the leading plants here is
the roller mills, who turn out each day

in the neighborhood of 600 barrels of meal and 400 barrels of flour, and on account of the growth of this business their capital has been increased.

The manufacturing of candy is a growing enterprise here. It is gaining in prosperity and increasing in importance. Some seasons of the year the plant is forced to work both day and night and their output is distributed throughout this state, part of Texas, Louisiana, etc.

In spite of the hard times the local furniture factory, which is now in operation, has been gaining and the issue for the year has been satisfactory to its owners. Their trade has grown to such an extent that it was necessary to enlarge its capacity and it is now on the road to success.

Among our large manufacturies are those engaged in cooperage, making of staves, handles, headings, etc., and while as a rule are not thought to have made a great deal during 1896, at the same time seem to have held their own. In some of these plants there is a large amount invested and shipments are made from these different enterprises to as far west as California, and as far east as the Atlantic seaboard.

The many other small manufacturies who are engaged in the manufacture of tobacco, wagons, carriages, mattresses, trunks, etc., are believed to have made a good living, besides some of them have made a little money.

Many consumers who are not close observers have asked how a city of this size has been able to sustain itself during the hard times which we have been experiencing, and the answer is made that if they would stop long enough to observe they would find out that Little Rock has a great many more manufactories than she has been given credit for, and these in themselves have in a great measure, assisted in giving Little Rock what prestige she now enjoys. It is true we need more of them and encouragement should be given to manufacturers who come here to seek locations, and with more railroads we would soon have a city of double the amount of its present population.

Within the last decade in appearance Little Rock has improved wonderfully. In the years of 1885 and 1886 she had but few paved streets: now she has many miles of paved and improved streets and the general character of the buildings, residences, etc., are much more substantial and attractive and for it size will compare most favorably with any in the Union and its geographical situation and its close proximity to coal beds and many other advantages ought to make this city a leading manufacturing center in the great Southwest.

Immigration bureau· have been turning their attention toward Arkansas and the tide of immigrants seems to be coming this way, for during the last five years many immigrants have bee locating in large numbers, in different portions of the state; and the class that has been seeking homes in our midst is thrifty and industrious. The beneficial results from this source is gradually but surely being felt.

In summarizing your questions, will say while 1896 in many respects so far as the net issues and results are concerned is not satisfactory, yet our city has held its own and in a measure we are better off than some sections who have been retrograding, and taken as a whole we have much for which to be thankful.

It is almost too early to prophesy in regard to 1897. The entire country has been in the throes of financial disasters during 1896, and the country at the present time is like a weak individual who has been through a siege of sickness and s in a convalescence state; and is compelled to gain more strength before he can walk. This is the present condition of the country and we hope it will not be long before the country is on its feet again. No one can expect it to jump at once from a long siege of depression into a state of prosperity. This will come gradually. Our lumber industries anticipate an increased demand for lumber to be shiped and distributed north, east and west. This together with our fruit crop will be a beneficial help and to tide over until the next fall crops are made; therefore conservative authorities while they do not look for a large spring trade they anticipate a very fair one and with the trade of next fall Arkansas hopes to be at lea t in a fairly prosperous condition.

WILLIAM P. HUTTON.

EDUCATION IN ARKANSAS.

By Prof. Junius Jordan, State Superintendent f Public Instruction.

The effort to make effectively prominent the material resources of Arkansas. has nullified to some extent, interest in her educational activities. The rush for timber and mining lands and for expositions of physical products has almost exceeded the bounds of moderation, and the writers have been kept busy in setting intensity to these inviting advantages. The quiet and effectual progress of our public and private school system, the personal self-sacrifice of our citizens, in this behalf, have largely been overlooked.

But a reaction i· beginning, and the silent, though steady energies of our people, through sunshine and storm, and amidst adversity as wel: as prosperity, are being appreciated in the presence of an advancing and praiseworthy devotion to higer and more permanent educational development. The West, once estimated in its importance by its trees, its expansive areas, its water courses, and its rustic sturdiness, is now at the front in a far more ennobling attitude and expression. Its newspapers, its pulpits, its comercial workers, its statesmen, have awakened a new enthusiasm in the student of progress. The observer, too, is called to close thought when he sees that this people, under a long series of adversities and a continuous cloud of unfair distrust and suspicion, have presented to the eye of the republic, entertaining, instructive and commanding results. When we think of the four years of devastating war, followed by nine years of negative conditions under the blight of reconstruction, and turn to look at the standards attained in the years that have ended with 1896, we almost disbelieve the existence of any other than a continued series of prosperous epochs. It seems however, that our state in this respect, furnishes a bright example of that exalted band that has "come up through great tribulation." and we present for consideration her attainments and successes in intellectual and moral development.

Other states may present more enlarged and comprehensive systems and accomplishments, but there were not the same advertisities and discouragements to meet and to overcome. When man contemplates attainments, his appreciation is measured by a knowledge of the obstacles surmounted, and the difficulties overcome in reaching the result.

Measuring the status of Arkansas today by this standard, as to her intellectual progress and achievements, we are willing to risk our standing for the benedictions that ever rest upon those who have fought a good fight.

The records show as follows: Enumeration of school population in 1895, 448,941; in 1896, 456,736.

Amounts received from tate tax, district tax, poll tax and other sources in 1895, $1,599,257.70; in 1896, $1,675,991.13.

Expenditures for salaries and other purposes in 1894-95, $1,130,232.75; in 1895-96, $1,232,986.08.

The amount unexpended in 1896 in the hands of various county treasurers, $443,005.05.

The permanent school fund was $450,-000 invested in Arkansas state bonds, on which there is an accumulated interest of $390,000. and an annual increase of $35,000.

In addition to the 5,980 schools taught. the state maintains the Arkansas Industrial University at Fayetteville; and likewise the Branch Normal College at Pine Bluff, the latter for colored teachers. The amounts annually expended for hese institutions averages $60,350.

Furthermore, the sum of $20.000 was appropriated by the Legislature in 1895. to maintain a normal school of one month in each year, in each county of the state. The success of this movement shows that 5,779 teachers out of 6,673 attended these normals.

There is in attendance at the public schools in the state 296,600 pupils, and at the State University 621; at the Branch Normal School, 100 students; at private nd denominational schools, 2,2200.

These are most encouraging exhibits of the financial and intellectual progress of Arkansas, as far as concerns the spirit of enterprise in her public and private schools. But, there is another most gratifying presentation to make, which establishes beyond question the sincerity as well as the sacrifices our people have made and are still making in behalf of our sons and aughters. We submit herewith a statement showing the amount of funds invested in private schools and in denominational institutions.

The figures include the values of buildings, grounds, and equipments of every nature, such as libraries. apparatus, furniture, etc.

Stuttgart College, Stuttgart, $6,000.

Jonesboro Training School. Jonesboro, $5,673.75.

Hinemon University, Monticello, $7,-150.

Rogers Academy, Rogers, $30,000.

Central Baptist Female College, Conway, $35,000.

Hiram and Lydia College Altus. $22,-100.

Arkadelphia Methodist College. Arkadelphia. $58,000.

Mountain Home Baptist College. Mountain Home, $13,000.

Quitman College, Quitman, $27,000.

Hope Institute, Hope, $7,500.

Bentonville College, Bentonville, $10,-500.

Conference Training School. Fordyce, $4,400.

Hendrix College, Conway, $62,000.

Arkadelphia Baptist College, Arkadelphia, $80,000.

Searcy Female Institute, Searcy, $80,-?00.

Searcy Male College, Searcy, $20,000.

Galloway Female College, Searcy, $45,-000.

Little Rock Academy, Little Rock, $7,-
000.

Arkansas Cumberland College, Clarks-
ville, $58,300.

Warner Female College, Little Rock,
$7,000.

Philadelphia High School, Melbourne,
$15,000.

Sulphur Rock Academy, and James-
town Academy, $2,500.

Arkansas College, Batesville, $30,000.

Little Rock University, Little Rock.

This shows an aggregate of $547,623.75
that has been invested in enterprises of
a private and denominational character
all in behalf of advanced intellectual
culture. The good people of this state,
in addition to the public school tax,
which they readily pay, state and district, through a spirit of love and en-
thusiastic devotion to mental and moral
development, have contributed of their
own private means and hard-earned resources over a half million of dollars
to the great cause of education. Nor
have we included in the above enumeration quite a number of other smaller
institutions, whose value would swell
the above sum to 550,000.

The record is before the people, and it
is one of which every one in Arkansas
should be proud and doubly encouraged
to continue faithful in this grand work
until our state sets the pace for a new
era in grander and nobler accomplishments in the great future of the Republic.

LETTER FROM MASSACHUSETTS.

Northborough, Mass., Dec. 26, 1896.

To the Editor of The Gazette.

I notice that you propose to issue a
January 15th edition, one feature of
which, I presume, will be cheap coal—
the foundation of the power of modern
civilization. I am told that you can secure good coal for manufacturing purposes delivered at $1.25 per ton. This
seems to us very low, and certainly will
attract capital and skilled labor, but
cautious men will inquire if a moderate
demand will increase the price.

Making and moving, creating and carrying, are the principles which lie at
the foundation of success. Mining and
agriculture are great sources of produc-
tion as well as manufacture. But,
however much we may produce, it
avails little unless we can transport it
to a good market. Good transportation
facilities can only be supported by ample material to be carried, and good
markets can only be found for articles
that can be afforded at small cost. Pro-
duction and transportation must go hand
in hand. Making and moving, creating and carrying, must be carefully ad-

justed on to the other so that there wil l
be harmony between the two great
forces.

This harmony is not to be secured by
mere guess-work. The subject must
be carefully studied by experts and men
whose only interest i- that of the public.
I am therefore glad to notice that you
are agitating the subject of creating a
railroad commission in Arkansas. About
twenty-five years ago we formed such
a commission in Massachusetts and
though we now have much to complain
of the information gathered and the ad-
vice given to contending parties—for
the powers of the commi-sion have always been merely advisory—have been
worth many times their cost. No
wrong method can long survive a full
statement of its evils by a disinterested
and competent tribunal.

The public interest is further protected al' over the country by the inter-
state commission. Mo-t of the states,
I presume, have railroad commissions.
and one great result is to prevent the
building of unnecessary railroads. I
notice recently that a piece of railroad
has been declared unnecessary in a
prosperous manufacturing neighborhood in Connecticut. The rail- will be
take up, and the stations and bridges
be sold. There have been several such
cases, and one of them only a very few
miles from my home. was a finely bui't
road that is now, and has been for
twenty years, totally abandoned. In
some form the public has to pay for
this. A wrongly located railroad is a
to'al lo-s. A properly located railroad
may be very poorly built, and meet
with great difficulties at the outset, but
with reasonab e management, it will become good property.

The main lines of railroad connecting principal points are mapped out
without much difficulty and details
must be left to the civil engineers, but
the connecting and cross lines present
many points that must be carefully
considered by experts in other depart-
ments than engineering. Then, too. the
ubject of street railways is under the
supervision of our railroad commission,
and this is a very important feature of
their duties now that electric and pneu-
matic methods of conveying power seem
to wholly supercede the use of horses.
For many reasons, therefore, I hope the
coming year wil witness the organization of a competent railroad commi-sion
in your state formed of gentlemen who
appreciate how grand a work is before
them in adapting all the latest improvements to the development of the resources of your great state. Faithfully
yours, CHARLES W. FELT.

POTTERIES IN ARKANSAS.

Little Rock as Adapted to Such Industries.

(By Wm. S. Thomas.)

Of the many industries for whose introduction Arkansas offers unusual inducements, there are none equaling the manipulation of our clays. Pottery is one of the oldest arts, its records antedate the birth of our Savior by more than 3000 years, and its products have been used by every nation of the earth civilized and savage. At the present time, with our advanced civilization, the demand has increased with the improvement and facilities for manufacture.

It is not the design of this article to give a history of pottery, or to explain the modes of manufacture of what comes under the head of the ceramic art, but to call the attention of those interested in this industry to the fact that within the boundaries of this state we have every variety of clay and other minerals used in the manufacture of ware, from building, paving, and fire brick, drain and sewer pipe, salt-glazed stoneware, yellow and Rockingham, C. C., and white granite ware, in short up to and including Severes china with the exception of feldspar, and of that I will speak farther on. It is doubtful if there is a locality in the world where, within the same area, all the raw material used in manufacturing the articles included in the term ceramics, is found in such close proximity as in this state and the near vicinity of Little Rock.

Except feldspar, there is not one ingredient lacking that enters into the composition of any known ware. Feldspar has been found in this state, but not of a purity that would answer for the higher grades of ware, though we have hopes a better quality will yet be discovered. It is found of excellent quality in the Indian Territory and Alabama. As this mineral is only used in limited quantities in the better classes of wares and for glasses, its absence is not serious, as will be seen from the fact that Staffordshire, England, where 200,000 people are employed in this industry, and the output annually amounts to $20,000,000, of which a large portion comes to the United States, gets most of its feldspar from this country, in Middletown, Conn.

Trenton, N. J., the Staffordshire of America, has twenty or more manufactories, which are not only obliged to send away for their feldspar, but to Pennsylvania for coal, and to South Carolina for their kaolin. Cincinnati has a number of potteries in successful operation—one whose ware competes with the finest made in Europe—but there is neither coal, or any ingredient, entering into the wares there manufactured, that is found in the near vicinity of that city. A thorough investigation has proved that no place in this country or Europe possesse, as many advantages for the prosecution of this industry in all its branches, as Arkansas. We have three varieties of coal, which will be found a very important item—we have seggar and fire brick clays, bal clay (so termed by the Stafford·hire potteries), kaolin, the purest of quartz, clay for terra cotta, stoneware, etc., in fact, for everything used in this art.

To the investor, this industry possesses advantages over most state·, as no amount of capital is invested in raw material—when wanted you go and dig it—no insurance on raw material, no danger of depreciation of value from time or any other cause, nor are the products affected by climate, time or fashion. For the manufacture of pottery in all its branches, Little Rock offers the advantage of cheap raw material, cheap labor, cheaper buildings than at the north, and has the farther advantage of an unlimited market with no near competition. It is hoped this article wi l meet the eye of some party sufficiently skilled in the art to appreciate these conditions, and take advantage of the situation.

The writer has given facts from personal experience, having been interested for a number of year· in one of the most extensive manufactories of the kind in the United States, and has made a practical test of many Arkansas clays. He would be pleased to give farther information to aid anyone wishing to investigate with a view to establishing a pottery.

In connection with clays, I wish to call attention to a mineral clo ely re-ated to kaolin or china clay, called bauxite. In the arts, this mineral is of late introduction, attention first being called to it as an oxide of alumina in 1868, and it is used for producing that metal and alum. It takes its name from Baux, in France, where it was first discovered. Thousands of tons are annually consumed in Philadelphia, Syracuse, Buffalo, and Brooklyn, for the manufacture of alum. North Carolina, Georgia, Alabama and Arkan as are the only states where this mineral has been found in commercial quantities, and the three first named states are at the present time supplying the market. The Arkansas deposits are quite extensive, of excellent quality, and are located from six to thirty miles from Little Rock. There i no reason why Little Rock should not at least manufacture alum, if not the metal.

REPORT OF LITTLE ROCK BOARD OF TRADE.

(By Geo. G. Harkness, Secretary.)

All things considered the business and ndu trial interests of the city of Little Rock are in better shape at the beginning of the current year than they have been at any time since the commercial barometer began falling four years ago. It is true that Little Rock, like every other city in the country, has suffered numerous failures during the late depression, but the percentage has been small by compar son with other places of equal commercial importance and few of her peers can hope to keep pace with her in the march of advancement that is now commencing, for the reason that the diversity of Little Rock's resources when money is easy, is exceptional.

As compared with 1895 the year just ended hows a slight advantage in a bus ness way. There were fewer failures in 1896 than in 1895 and these were for the most part failures of concerns that in 1895 were weak and due to fail but which struggled into the succeeding year with an effort only to succumb finally. As to value and volume of busine s the best criterions are found on comparative freight, express and postoffice figures and bank clearings. A compar son of freight receipts for the last three months of 1895 and 1896 shows the startling increase of 3737 cars in the latter year, due to the protecting influence of the Little Rock Board of Trade. Following is the statement by month:

	1895. cars.	1896. cars.
October	2762	4292
November	2832	3704
December	2842	4177
	8436	12,173
Increase in 1896		3737

A comparison of bank clearings shows an increase as follows:

1895	$16,202,706
1896	16,304,815
Increa e in 1896	$102,109

The gross receipts of the Little Rock postoffice for the fiscal year ending June 30, 1896, were nearly the same as in the preceding year:

1895	$ 58,207.01
1896	58,462.16
Increase n 1896	$255.15

The receipts of the Pacific Express Company, the only company doing busines here, were somewhat smaller in 1896 than in 1895.

Though no very determined effort was

made during the past year to attract to this city new industrial plants, the Board of Trade managed in a quiet way to add a spoke and hub factory, employing twenty-five hands, to the woodworking interests of the city and to install here a first-class tobacco manufactory. This concern is called the Arkanas Tobacco Works, it manufactures plug and twist of a superior quality and has been particularly successful. It employs an average of thirty hands.

The cotton interests of Little Rock have suffered seriously during the current cotton year, owing to the destruction on September 16, 1896, of the mammoth East Little Rock press of the Union Compress Company. This was the largest building of the kind in the world and its immense storage capacity greatly facilitated the handling of cotton on this market. All cotton handled on the local market since the destruction of the East Little Rock press was pressed at the North Little Rock Compress, but the limited capacity of this press caused much cotton to be diverted from this market. The low price of cotton this season has prevented several thousand bales stored in and around Little Rock from coming into sight. Following is a statement of the cotton movement on the Little Rock market for the cotton season of 1895 and 1896, from September 1, t December 31:

Receipts, Sept. 1 to Dec. 31.
1895..... 75,300
1896.... 69,006
Shipments Sept. 1 to Dec. 31.
1895 54,342
1896....:... 58,746
Stock, Dec. 31.
189...5................ 21,801
1896......... 9,500

On December 31, 1896, middling was quoted at 6c on the Board of Trade and on the corresponding day of the previous year at 7 1-4c

The business men of Little Rock are at present united as never before in a determined effort to advance the commercial interests of Little Rock and Arkanas from the inside. The Little Rock Board of Trade has inaugurated a a special feature of its work for 1897 a series of citizens' meetings. It is intended that the business men shall get together at least once each month, touch elbows and exchange ideas for the good of the community. Two of these meetings have already been held and such a spirit of pride in the city and state shown and such an enthusiasm for development as cannot fail to work out great benefits. Already plans are on foot looking to the building of "Greater Little Rock." These plans were formulated at the two meetings referred to and the activity with which the business men of the community have taken hold, determined to do their share in the trenches has fired much new material with an ambition to participate. The committee appointed to secure the convention of Arkansas Teachers for Little Rock has earned the first laurel wreath by closing with the executive committee of the Southern Teachers' Association for the holding of the convention in Little Rock in June next. This committee consists of Prof. T. L. Cox, Mr. W. S. Mitchell and Mr. Geo. Russ Brown.

The entire power of the Little Rock Board of Trade will be thrown into an effort to increase the railway mileage of the state of Arkansas during 1897, to this end the Legislature will be urged to pass the Naylor bill, embodying the opinions of the legislative committee of the Board of Trade and providing for the construction of railroads within the state by convict labor.

Among the certain factors that will contribute to the comfort and prosperity of Little Rock are the new free bridge across the Arkansas river at the foot of Main street and the new pressed brick plant which will be built in the West End by Lieper & Apperson. An almost certain consequence of the completion of the new bridge is the construction of an electric line connecting the Army Post with Little Rock and embracing North Little Rock.

It is hardly possible that another year will go by without active work being commenced on the extension of the Little Rock and Memphis railroad west from Little Rock to Wister Junction. The Little Rock and Mississippi railroad, commonly known as the Worthen road, has just been turned over to Mr. Chas. F. Penzel as receiver for the evident purpose of closing the eighteen-mile gap that remains between its present terminus and Little Rock. The Kansas City, Pittsburg and Gulf railroad has nearly completed the stretch of line between Fort Smith and Texarkana and will probably build on to Hot Springs and Little Rock from Mena, Ark. Arrangements have been completed for the extension of the Corbin road from Sunnyside to Hamburg in Ashley county.

The movement of the Board of Trade of Little Rock for increased railway mileage has struck a responsive chord throughout the state, and in view of the determined pull and the pull together that is being made, it is safe to assert that something is bound to come.

The lumber business of the state, which means more to Arkansas and Little Rock than any one interest except possibly cotton, has already received a very considerable stimulus on the prospect of its protection by legislative action under the incoming national administration.

In conclusion, the people of Little Rock owe much to the patriots who have kept intact the Little Rock Board of Trade during the late depression and who have by their membership and support builded it up to what it now is, the strongest commercial organization that ever represented the business interests of Little Rock. The Board of Trade is alive to the opportunities which now lie open to Little Rock and every business man should feel it his duty to join this good organization and help push things along.

9 7 8 3 3 3 7 4 1 9 4 9 3